MOONSCAPE

11/18/21

All the best,
Randy

MOONSCAPE

Randall T. Elliott

Captain, United States Army

Copyright © 2014 by Randall T. Elliott.

Library of Congress Control Number: 2013922786
ISBN: Hardcover 978-1-4931-5371-8
Softcover 978-1-4931-5370-1
eBook 978-1-4931-5372-5

All rights reserved. No part of this book may be reproduced or transmitted in any form or by any means, electronic or mechanical, including photocopying, recording, or by any information storage and retrieval system, without permission in writing from the copyright owner.

Print information available on the last page.

Rev. date: 12/26/2013

To order additional copies of this book, contact:
Xlibris
1-888-795-4274
www.Xlibris.com
Orders@Xlibris.com
102866

CONTENTS

Prologue 7
Introduction 9
Reflections 11

Chapter 1   The Long Journey 13
Chapter 2   The Face of the Moon 31
Chapter 3   Men Die Hard 42
Chapter 4   Diminutive Men, Lion-Sized Hearts 49
Chapter 5   Who is Charlie? 54
Chapter 6   The Institutionalization of Death 61
Chapter 7   MEDCAP 67
Chapter 8   Fear of Fear 74
Chapter 9   The Mystery of the Iron Triangle 80
Chapter 10   What an Air Strike Means to Me 88
Chapter 11   Booby Traps and Hungry Men 93
Chapter 12   A Moment in a Firebase 102
Chapter 13   A Fleeting Moment, a Death 109
Chapter 14   With Allies Like These 112
Chapter 15   To Kill the Thoughtless 116
Chapter 16   Of Rome Plows and Agent Orange 129
Chapter 17   A Day in Vietnam 133
Chapter 18   Slaughter at Soui Tre 141
Chapter 19   A Night Spent on Buffalo Dung 149
Chapter 20   In a Foxhole Full of Water 154
Chapter 21   The Look of Death 159
Chapter 22   Jackson Goes Down 163
Chapter 23   C Rations and Life in the Bush 168
Chapter 24   Of Snakes and Men 177

Chapter 25	A Line of Sweating Infantrymen	180
Chapter 26	Watch Out for VC	186
Chapter 27	Tet, Bloody Tet	196
Chapter 28	A Friend Dies	209
Chapter 29	Murder from the Sky	213
Chapter 30	One More Time	219
Chapter 31	The Shot Hits Home	225
Chapter 32	Goin' Home	235
Chapter 33	Last Patrol	242

Epilogue 243

PROLOGUE

The infantry
I was proud of what I was.
I was the infantry, I was this country.
My sweat was its rivers, my blood was its rain.

We shared our pain, we shared our loss.
We were not brave, we harbored fear like no others.
We did what our country asked of us.
We gave our best. We did what we thought was right.
We tried our hardest.

We thought of home often.
We died without fanfare, without glory; no one was watching, no bands were playing.

Those who came back from the jungle will always be different men.
But we will always be brothers. We will always be proud Americans.

INTRODUCTION

These are the reflections of a patriotic young officer who volunteered to fight in the infantry during America's war in Vietnam. Wanting to fight the evil of communism and do right by all he knew, this Southern soldier's first thought when jumping from a helicopter into the tall grass of a field in Vietnam on his first air assault operation was "I'm the ultimate extension of American foreign policy, and I'm here to execute that policy, by God." Full of patriotism and the invincibility of youth, Elliott wanted to fight. He wanted to do America's bidding against our enemies. The Russians were the main antagonists, the enemy of his generation, but the enemy in Vietnam would do.

Then as the days and weeks went by, a voice of doubt began to speak louder and louder as the shadow of disillusionment crept in. Later, as the months went by, he would descend into a nightmare of despair and pain as men died needlessly and in vain, and others were shattered in mind and body. Squandered valor and wasted sacrifices would eat at his soul, right up to the breaking point and beyond.

Follow me then into Dante's *Inferno*, a special kind of hell where you are alone, you are isolated, and you do not know why you are there. But you **are** there, and death, maiming, and a panoply of hideous events await your every move, your every breath. It may not happen today, but it probably will tomorrow. You have yourself and those few around you. You have been forsaken by your country and condemned to the valley of the shadow of death by those politicians who knew not what they were doing. There is nothing and no one to light or guide your way. You are not on a crusade. There are no grand parades, and no one can see you. No one will buy bonds to win the war; no one really cares. For some, even their families betrayed them. You are now, as General Sherman said, in hell.

Walk with me then in the footsteps of the infantry.

REFLECTIONS

It had been less than two years after I first put on the American Army uniform that I found myself in the steamy jungles and rancid rice paddies of Vietnam, a steely-eyed killer. Elite forces such as the 101st Airborne Division are sometimes called such semiderogatory terms. My experiences in the war deeply etched in my mind how I would view the United States, what we were trying to do, and what was going wrong. From the perspective of a frontline officer in the thick of the fighting in Vietnam, I hope to present a glimpse of what many of us were about: patriotism, unrestricted faith in our system and in the people who represented it, the concept of duty, the value of honor, and, beneath it all, the unspoken foundation of mental and physical courage. We would carry on the traditions of our fathers who fought the Second World War, no matter the circumstances.

I also was from the South and had a full repertoire of Southern values, having had two great-grandfathers in Robert Lee's Army of Northern Virginia. This too was part of the cultural heritage that went to war in Vietnam with me. Later it would become all too apparent that our faith in the system had been misplaced. Somewhat similar to that of our forefathers. We were willing to sacrifice and, if necessary, ready to die for our country, our families, and our way of life, if need be. None of us wanted to die for a pointless, ill-conceived abstraction such as the domino theory or some other half-baked concept. We simply wanted to do the right thing, and to the airborne, kicking communist ass was the right thing. We were gung ho and ready to do any reasonable thing our country asked of us. We felt like we could conquer the world if need be.

Ultimately, we had been misled or wrongly directed not by mean-spirited people, but by people who simply did not understand what they were doing. They had no fundamental grasp of the struggle that was then taking place in South Asia. They did not have the moral courage to exact the truth, a task that would be sadly left to the citizen youth of the United States, both those fighting and those protesting.

Under the fervor of an anticommunist crusade, we were thrust into the middle of a Vietnamese civil war. True, there was anemic support for the Vietcong from China and the USSR but far less support than the U.S. was providing for South Vietnam. The U.S. was sending money, materiel, and, above all, men. In the years ahead, both sides of the Cold War would up the ante, but it was the U.S. who would become the most involved and pay the greatest price.

Many of the people who sent soldiers to Vietnam would later walk away from the issue when it became divisive and go on to carve out fine careers in government or to enrich themselves in various civilian careers. The worst opportunists would even deny that they had ever held such views (when they became unpopular) when those views fell from fashion and would no longer serve their personal ambitions. Others would view the war and their participation in it seriously and perhaps be bothered to some degree by what their miscalculations and lack of prescience eventually wrought. Their miscalculations would forever change how Americans viewed and trusted their government. However, for those of us who fought in that brutal war, it would not be something we could ever walk away from. We would all be wounded for the rest of our lives in one way or another. A popular slogan I saw right after the war ended perfectly captured the essence of this situation in saying that "all gave some, and some gave all."

CHAPTER 1

THE LONG JOURNEY

I had just turned six years old. I was playing on the floor with my first cousin Maxie decorating a Christmas tree at his house. My father and my much-revered uncle Steve were watching the news on the relatively new or at least newly available invention called television in Steve's living room. I could tell by their voices and that of the newscaster that events were not happy, and people were worried. Uncle Steve was tall, a fireman in my hometown, and respected by all. He did not appear to have the consuming flaws and disgraceful behavior of my father.

The Russians were blockading Berlin, threatening to seize the city and confront American troops. The clouds of war hung heavily over Europe once again. Korea was mentioned also, and Dad and Uncle Steve had a long discussion about where Korea was, since neither knew for sure. They eventually decided it was somewhere near China. About then, Maxie and I were getting noisy and tired, squabbling as youngsters do. My father was preparing to leave, and I had become attentive when Uncle Steve said, "Well, it looks like there is going to be another war. I guess we will find out what kind of men Maxie and Randy will be when they grow up, because they will have to fight the Russians."

I was thunderstruck. At the age of six, I had been given life instructions, my first set of orders. I had just been made a soldier by the man I most revered in the world. Tall, handsome, and fatherly in advice and demeanor, my uncle had issued me a direct challenge, an order. It was as if God had spoken. It would be me against the Russians. I had heard of Japs, Germans, and some others, but the name Russians sounded strange, if not funny to my youthful ears. Who were these people? Where did they live? I still was not sure where Germany was, but I knew the Japs lived on a big island somewhere. Who would be the Russian I would have to fight? Would he be bigger or stronger or braver than I was supposed to be? I soon scoured books to find out what they looked like. They had strange names, Ivan and Vasiliy.

My future had been laid out; it was clear. It was also starkly clear that my father and uncle hated Russians with an intensity that I did not understand. It all had something to do with politics. Nevertheless, I would fight those despicable people who, according to Uncle Steve, wanted to enslave us with their insane, corrupt system and its brutal apparatus. He said they were worse than the Japs and Nazis of the last war, and that was good enough for me.

It was not something comprehensible to a six-year-old, but later came the realization that Uncle Steve probably would not have remembered what he said even an hour afterward. I had asked Maxie* the next day, and he didn't remember. Years later, as a father, I would remember that incident over and over again and weigh very carefully what advice I offered to my two beautiful young daughters.

*Maxie went on to have a successful career as a civil servant in the U.S. Army and would retire in the mid-1990s, returning to the hometown where we both grew up.

Early Training for the Journey

Time passed quickly. I grew up in the comfortable climate of Florida, in the relaxed, almost-pressure-free era of the Eisenhower years. Major preoccupations of my youth in this idyllic setting were going to the beach—said to be one of the world's best—or fishing, hunting, and a myriad of other activities that could even make a Huck Finn jealous. However, coming from a dirt-poor family, we had little income. I started to work at the age of eleven, delivering papers by bicycle for three hours a day on a long route through my small hometown. This brought in limited funds, enough for me to proudly present the first television to my family at the age of twelve.

During these formative years, I began to read war books and go to war movies when my earnings and time permitted. All the men around me had been in the Big One, and it was thrilling to hear their stories. It seemed to me to be a very courageous thing, and they all said I'd grow up and have my war too. Sitting at the edge of the bar in the American Legion Hall, where my dad would perch me, I could hear the alcohol-embellished accounts of shooting down Jap planes and killing Krauts. The setting made no difference. What mattered was what I heard, and it was the gospel.

As I got older, I sought out these veterans, neighborhood men who had been in combat in World War II and Korea, and asked all kinds of questions about what they had done. What were their experiences, how had they reacted, and what was their general impression of their experiences? It was sometimes difficult to extract complete information, and some would not speak of their experiences at all, but most would impart some idea of what they had been through. A few were flattered that a kid was interested. Slowly, a mental picture of what would be expected of me later began to form. I began to fantasize about being brave and saving other soldiers or escaping from a prisoner of war camp, and I felt both excitement and trepidation about such prospects. My training had begun.

Within two years of giving me the inadvertent orders, Uncle Steve died. His son Maxie went to school out of state, and we slowly lost contact. I often thought of that day and wondered what had become of my cousin.

By the time I was in high school, football became a major interest for me and an unusual learning experience. It was a good place to settle scores and learn how to function as part of a team. During a game in the eleventh grade, a coach once yelled at me to "put it on the line" since he thought I was not playing hard enough. In the next play, I knocked an opposing running back unconscious; and when the game was over, I was expecting to be chastised but heard, "Randy, that was as good and fair as a hit could be, and I'm really proud of you." I felt like I could almost fly. Here I was being rewarded for being part of a team, hitting hard, and being told by a coach that he was proud was the praise I never heard from my father.

On the football field, it did not matter who your parents were or if you were from any particular part of town. What mattered was that you tackled well, knew your position, and developed a solid teamwork ethic. The skills I learned on the football field would serve me well in later years. I learned to master fear and to use physical strength in a productive way and as part of a larger effort. I liked the contact, hearing helmets crack and pads hit, the sweat. In many ways, it was a level playing field. As a bonus, you were praised for controlled violence. It was my first experience in this world, and while I did not know it then, it would also be part of my training.

Schoolwork seemed simple enough. But differences between me and others began to surface. Being poor and with now-divorced parents, I was shunned by many. My father was an alcoholic and an embarrassment to his children.

He earned little or no money and offered no support. Dad would drift off for months at a time, leaving neither a clue as to where he was nor a cent to assist his family. He had been a brilliant man who had worked in the Green Cove Springs naval shipyard during World War II. He rose from apprentice welder to shipyard foreman during those heady days. He had devised a method of installing turret race rings (the circular rail that shipboard guns rotated on) that shaved a considerable time off ship construction. He had even received a letter of congratulations from President Roosevelt for helping the war effort. It was the only job of any substance he would ever hold. Alcohol overtook him, destroyed his superb mental faculties, and eventually his health. He died at the age of fifty-nine. In the time I knew him, he never uttered a single word of encouragement or fatherly advice, much less any trace of compassion or love.

When my teen years came along, some girls were not allowed to associate with me, much less go out with someone that was so obviously poor white trash, as people in our economic predicament in the South were called. I tried not to let class distinctions bother me since there was nothing I could do about it. I did say to myself that I would continue to work hard and eventually make something of myself, make a mark. My only recourse was to believe that in the United States, you could actually do such a thing. It seemed a birthright; one did not even have to question it.

I graduated from high school in the spring of 1959 and headed for college. I had, by luck with my family background, obtained an appointment to West Point but was disqualified after failing the physical exam for being color blind. After that disappointment, an academic scholarship at Stetson University in Florida had come my way, enabling me to fulfill one of my dreams. I could at least get a college education, which seemed to be a sure ticket to a better future. But it would be necessary for me to work at several jobs during my college years since the scholarship defrayed only some two-thirds of costs. It was also very apparent that luxuries such as fraternities, cars, and spring-break trips would be out of the question. I had no real idea of what to expect, but I was determined to be the first college graduate in my family.

So college began, and I had to study hard to make up for coasting in high school. I took mostly science and engineering courses and then a heavy dose of political science, graduating with a dual major. After four years, which now seem like a distant blur, graduation neared. During those hectic years, I had worked in the library and for a pest control company. I had been a dormitory counselor, a cook in the cafeteria, an assistant to the dean of men, and a reader to a blind man. I had several other part-time jobs to augment my limited scholarship, but they were more the odd job, handyman types. Each job, no matter how menial, taught me lessons, let me try leadership techniques or hone some other skill, and, most especially, taught me how to work with other people. It was a useful complement to the more formal education of college.

Of course, in the early 1960s, I had also been in the Reserve Officers' Training Corps or ROTC. During this time, the question was not *if* you would join the military after high school or college. The question was simply what service—army, navy, air force, or marines. Coming from a family that had answered the call to serve from as far back as Robert E. Lee's Confederates and the American Revolution, I simply never thought of not entering the military to do my share. It was just a part of our culture. I selected the army because I jokingly said I could walk farther than I could swim and said the same for the air force, in that I could walk farther than fly. In reality, I picked the army because I wanted to prove myself. I wanted to fight the enemies of the U.S. on personal terms, face-to-face.

In college, like on the football field, one's hometown and parents did not seem so important. I was elected president of *Scabbard and Blade*, an honorary military society in which soldierly bearing, academic standing, and military knowledge meant more than what side of town you came from. It was something I earned by performance and merit and had nothing to do with how I was evaluated by my parentage. Having never been born to anything and experienced shame and humiliation from my status in life, achieving goals in college was sweet indeed. I savored every moment, and to be honest, I looked for more ways to excel and be better than anyone else. Had I known the tests that were to come, I may have had second thoughts.

During my senior year, I was appointed to the rank of commander of the ROTC detachment. It was here that I could practice techniques of leadership and motivation. I learned the importance of being prepared, knowing what to do, and being in the lead. The first opportunity for public speaking came my way, and I delivered an address that got a standing ovation. Accomplished people were applauding the son of a drunk.

Before I graduated, it was evident that many unanticipated doors were open to me. There was a future out there, one filled with all kinds of opportunity, but another dream beckoned—the desire to serve my country—and it would come first. I felt that a patriotic debt was owed by me to this country (Uncle Steve had ensured that), and at least partial repayment was a duty and an obligation. My mother had also hinted, in her infrequent guidance lessons, that the military would be a good place for me.

On graduation day, I thought, *Uncle Steve, I'm almost there*. Soon after graduation, I put on the uniform I had been reaching for all those years. I was an eager volunteer who was ready to serve the country. That's what I wanted to do. I had come a long way to be an officer of the United States Army. I could not have been more proud, more anxious to do whatever my superiors and leaders could ask. I wanted to serve; I was even ready for war if need be. I almost looked forward to it. I had a score to settle with the enemies of the United States.

First Days in the Army

After college graduation the first excitement as a new soldier was the airborne school at Fort Benning, Georgia. The training program was a mere six weeks long, but they were difficult weeks, and the dropout rate for officers was high. We did a lot of physical training or PT, early morning long distance runs, countless push-ups, alerts at all times, and even more physical activity after that. Some of the most arduous PT stints were in the punji pits where you practiced bayonet fighting with a heavy stick, well padded on each end, and meant to simulate the size and weight of a rifle. This was usually followed by short tactical exercises, long marches, and hours of more exercise thrown in to keep us busy.

Gradually, we were introduced to packing parachutes and all of the specialized airborne training facilities at Fort Benning. The facilities included the notorious twenty-seven-foot tower, the two-hundred-foot drop tower, and a variety of other conditioning pieces of equipment. Each seemingly designed to torment even the strongest. Training in a correct parachute landing fall or PLF was the most intense since that part of a parachute drop is where the majority of injuries occur.

The seriousness of training for war began to permeate my mind. I thought of Normandy and other airborne operations of the past and realized that this was no game. The brutal, apparent truth being that if we go to war, men will die.

Once the training was near complete, our group was to make five live jumps from the large, four-engine C-130 troop transport aircraft. The first jump was a true lifetime experience since, as an officer, I headed a stick or line of paratroops out of the aircraft. This meant standing in the open door for what seemed like an hour, waiting for a red light to turn green, and that meant "go!" While out on the runway, waiting for aircraft for our second actual jump, we were ordered into formation and told that President Kennedy had been shot and was dying. We were formed into an ad hoc battalion, issued maps of Cuba, and carried out several tactical exercises, mostly involving fighting in cities. Some of the jumpmaster sergeants were sure we would be dropped on Cuba, and they paid special attention to training young second lieutenants such as myself for the fighting that they thought lay ahead.

I was not a political person, but to have our young president killed in such a disgusting way was so repulsive. We all felt helpless during those days and asked the why questions over and over. His death seemed so pointless and needless. This too would be a type of training for later events.

Our four additional jumps were postponed for about a week while the entire country mourned. By then, the political situation had calmed down somewhat, and President Kennedy's funeral was over. We were all still in a state of shock, and I remember thinking about Kennedy as I floated down from my second jump, during the minute or two you have of idyllic peace, before you crash into the ground.

Assignment: Germany. Face-to-Face with the Russians

After airborne and other special training, I was assigned to West Germany, just south of Frankfurt. This was it, what I had been waiting for. I was stationed near the Fulda Gap, a gently rolling plains area ideal for tank warfare and where the Russians would come through if they started a war. The Fulda Gap was the gateway into the central part of Germany, about seventy-five miles east of Frankfurt. We were told that we simply had to hold a few days if the Russians attacked, and help would arrive from the U.S. None of us, even second lieutenants, believed this. We were jokingly called speed bumps by other troops, and it seemed about right to us.

I arrived at Frankfurt/Main airbase on January 1, 1964, and saw my first snow. I met my escort and was driven in an open jeep (no windshield, this was considered tactical in the lingo of the day) to the training site at Baumholder. I was frozen, or at least felt that way. But being in Germany—in my first actual army unit—felt good, and a few weeks later, I got my initial orientation at the Fulda Gap. You could look across into East Germany with binoculars and see the enemy with his tanks, wire fences, and constant patrols. So eager to deal with our only real enemy, I felt like saying, "Come now. I don't want to miss dealing with you, sons of bitches." I did not want to miss the war I had been ordered to by Uncle Steve.

The Cold War was very real for us. Alerts were held once a month, frequently more often. Surprise alerts and inspections happened with a frequency that made them seem only a minor irritation. Training exercises—field duty—took about eight to nine months a year, leaving little time for normal garrison activity. All of us got used to eating army rations, living in tents, and the general conditions of field activity in Europe at the time. Marches, alerts, live-fire exercises, and exercises at the battalion, brigade, and even division level prepared us for what might be necessary if the Russians attacked. We were trained and well equipped, and in my view, we were a field army and would do well handling the Russians. The only thing we were really concerned about was numbers. They had us outnumbered heavily, but we had a certain arrogance and felt that numbers were of little importance since our equipment and morale were better, and we felt the West Germans would fight well on our side and tip the balance.

The periods of time in garrison were downright boring, getting ready for inspections, repair, and maintenance of equipment. There were all kinds of extra duty for young lieutenants, from payroll (paying the troops), giving lectures on venereal diseases, to being duty officer. Being a duty officer on weekends could almost simulate combat, as troops who went to local *gasthauses* drank too much, let off too much steam, and invariably got into all sorts of trouble. I got set up as a duty officer since I didn't know any better. It was New Year's Eve. One large mechanized unit had just come in from three months in the field, and our unit had been out for a month as well. In addition to that, troops were not normally paid in the field. So with a lot of cash, free time, and much to vent about, troops were turned loose for the holiday.

Too much liquor, too much field duty, and too much freedom led to a really upsetting situation in the *kaserne* (military barracks area in Germany). By 10:00 pm I had arrested over a dozen troops for drunk and disorderly conduct. By 11:00 pm, I had to call out an MP (military police) platoon. Just after that, while checking the NCO club (like the officer's club, sergeants have a club for their ranks as well), a thoroughly intoxicated sergeant staggered out of the club and started swinging at me. Two MPs made short work of the drunk (who would soon be a private first class for assaulting an officer), but it set the tone for the rest of the evening. By midnight (New Year's) or just after, I had declared the equivalent of martial law in the barracks, closed all clubs, and put over fifty men on duty to maintain order. By 6:00 am, over thirty soldiers were in the slammer, and things had calmed down.

I discovered later that my battalion commander wanted to "check me out" and see how I would handle such an event.

Later, when I briefed him on the events of the past twenty-four hours, he said I passed okay.

There was free time too, and the beer and German women were great. The dollar was still strong against the mark and even a lowly second lieutenant's salary was still very high in Germany. German women seemed to like the Americans, and we liked them. Although relations were limited by our condition, romances abounded. Some were simple sex and dating, a few got married, but all of us had a great time.

I volunteered for a duty that most young officers avoided since it was considered too risky for their future. I volunteered for and became a nuclear weapons control officer. Since one small accident or oversight could fail a unit's nuclear mission and could easily end your career. I don't know why I wanted the assignment, but others did not want it, and it was something I could prove. I thought I could do a good job, and it seemed like a position that would get some recognition if you did it right; but on the other hand, if you did not, it was the end of your career. I liked that aspect of my new job.

Nuclear weapons were stored in numerous locations, and each unit with nuclear weapons had storage, maintenance, and inspection responsibilities. They also had the mission of being prepared to deliver or fire these weapons in case of war.

Alerts and large military maneuvers were more exciting than life in garrison. You never knew if an alert was the real thing or not, and it was not our worry. Our mission was simple—be ready to do your job. When we had an alert, usually at 1:00 or 2:00 am, our little valiant band would quickly assemble and set off to our alert site. Once there, we would set up security and prepare to arm our nuclear weapons. If another series of correct numbers arrived over the radio, we would arm the weapons and prepare to deliver them. Only once did I feel that we would go that far, but then at the last moment, we were ordered to stand down. Such alerts were very intense and hard on the nerves, but it was good training if the real event ever happened.

Being in this position (my predecessor had been fired, which gave me an easy act to follow) gave me a small team to train, drill, and run as I liked, as long as the unit passed all tests with flying colors. The biggest test was the implied threat of war. If war came, the nuclear weapons in Germany had to be ready and available for use. And we had to be ready for any contingency, from the Russians including their using Spetznaz (special forces) troops (specially trained to attack U.S. nuclear storage sites) to local citizens who may sympathize with the Soviets.

The special training schools in Southern Germany lasted for almost three months. By the end, I was a qualified nuclear weapons proficiency officer. One of the more stressful tests called a technical proficiency inspection or TPI in military lingo was called right after I completed schooling. We passed the test, but I was not pleased since we had a number of small nagging errors. Errors could be costly, even small ones, so I concentrated on every imaginable situation and tried to anticipate every eventuality.

Our team was considered an elite element, and in order to keep the privileges the enlisted men had and to keep our standing high, we drilled and drilled; and seven months later, we were tested again. This time, to the surprise of the inspectors, we not only passed, but also did with the first perfect score in Europe. I was extremely proud of the team and felt we had all pitched in and done a good job, so I paid for the beer at the celebration we had that weekend. As a result of that test, I was called up to V Corps Headquarters as a nuclear weapons inspector. For the next two years, our inspection team roamed all over Europe, inspecting nuclear units, examining their storage facilities, watching them put nuclear warheads together, and examining how they went through their firing sequences. All the time I was garnering valuable experience, unaware of this important accrual most of the time.

Nuclear war, later an unthinkable nightmare, was given scarcely a thought by us. We were all conditioned and trained to think of nuclear weapons as just bigger than the artillery shells and bombs of World War II. We saw films of actual nuclear weapons being detonated, but we never saw any consequences such as the human damage. We had Soviet units, installations, headquarters, and training areas as targets, and that seemed perfectly justified. Our weapons were more accurate, more efficient, and would help address the asymmetries we faced in numbers. Nuclear war was just another obstacle to surmount. Any questions or restraint would have been viewed in the harshest terms. Those few in Germany (mostly Germans but a few Americans) who did complain were instantly labeled as bed wetters, professional worriers, and pinko fellow travelers.

My boss at the time, Brice Bell, had been in the Korean War and was a superb mentor. Since he had been in the infantry and fought the Chinese and North Koreans during the Korean War, he was a source of considerable knowledge and experience. With great patience, he guided me through various learning experiences with the skill of a gifted teacher. In Brice I saw the best qualities of an officer—honesty, leadership, courage, and integrity.

Each inspection we conducted seemed to have its own share of humor, danger, and alarm. Most of the units we inspected passed well, but some failed. Some would not have been able to do their mission—the greatest sin there is in the military. Anecdotes about various incidents abounded. One trooper fainted during a particularly difficult nuclear weapons assembly procedure; the stress and intensity were so great.

The most frightening incident came when a unit being tested dropped a nuclear weapon right on the ground and earned a failing grade. They had failed to properly check the cable on the hoist they were using, and while they lifted out the missile warhead, the cable snapped. Everybody hit the ground, laughing later at our combined stupidity. If the nuclear weapon had detonated, we would have been vaporized.

Another unit forgot a key sequence and actually threaded a bolt incorrectly (stripped the bolt) and failed. Anytime a unit failed, the commander was usually relieved from duty and replaced. This terminated a career, and such tests were not taken lightly.

The two years passed quickly and yet were full of learning, excitement, and problem-solving challenges. I had found a home in the army.

Clouds in the Distance

Every day on the military radio news network in Europe and in the *Stars and Stripes* (the highly edited, official military version of the news), we heard more and more ominous news from Vietnam. We were committing more troops to Vietnam every month, and units were being sent from all over the U.S. Replacements for units in Vietnam were starting to be pulled out of Europe at a noticeable rate and then later at an alarming rate. Soldiers would serve only twelve months in Vietnam unless they elected to stay longer, and this high rate of turnover was causing incredible turbulence in the army. Units that had been superb fighting machines in Germany were reduced to shells in a few months as all the experienced noncommissioned officers (or sergeants who are really the backbone of the army)*, and officers were pulled out for duty in Vietnam.

The overall effect of the fighting in Vietnam was just starting to have an impact on the psyche of the army in

Europe; it was already souring those who were coming back from the jungles of South Asia. They were not happy men and were spreading discord about what was happening in Asia. It was now fall 1966, and I received orders (even if you volunteer, in the army, you need orders to do anything) to return to the U.S. and join the 101st Airborne Division, which was now on alert for deployment to Vietnam. I was overjoyed and arranged to depart a month early to give myself more time to prepare for my duties, whatever they may be, with the 101st.

*Sergeants are enlisted men who have done well and gone up in rank, a process that sometimes takes years. They are naturally closer to the average soldier than officers. Officers are commissioned by Congress and do not have to serve as enlisted men, although some do and later get a commission via officer candidate school or in college ROTC. A good sergeant can be invaluable to a small unit. He can keep the officer from making fatal mistakes and help educate him. Sometimes there is friction between NCOs and officers, but if it is helpful, it is all right. Sometimes the chemistry does not work and transfers are in order. Nevertheless, sergeants are the backbone of the army, and their expertise and contributions cannot be over emphasized.

Preparing to Deploy

When I arrived at Fort Campbell, Kentucky, I went straight to Division Headquarters. The commanding general had been in Europe as a brigadier general while I was stationed there, and I had gotten to know him somewhat, even though I was a lieutenant at the time. I wrangled an appointment and had about thirty seconds to say hello and ask, actually plea, for a combat command—the more difficult, the better. If I was going to fight in Vietnam,

I wanted to be with the best, to be in the thick of things. Arrogance and overconfidence had come to the surface. I wanted to fight for my country. I was informed that a command would probably be available, and it would be one of the more difficult positions for a junior captain.

Initially, the company I would command would be part of the fire brigade for the division. This meant that we would be completely heliborne and called on to put out fires. I knew that in the sometimes-elliptical phraseology of the military, this really meant we would see a lot of combat, and we would be tossed into the fray when things were going badly for others—typically the lot of the airborne. To be trusted in such a position was an honor, and I felt nothing but pride and patriotism. I was very eager to get on with things. The Vietnamese were not Soviets, but we had been told there were communists invading Vietnam from the north, and that was more than good enough for me. I wanted to fight them. Uncle Steve's test was at hand.

Soon after arriving at my new command, I held a meeting with the company, introduced myself, and speculated about the interesting year ahead of us. I also said that I hoped we would be able to have a party—all of us—when we got back to this spot in just over a year. That sent up hoots and cheers, even though all of us in the infantry knew that the likelihood of every man returning was less than slim.

My company was made up of volunteers who passed rigorous physicals and are well aware of the rugged, tough legacy we have to live up to. Only volunteers are accepted in the airborne, and these men were superbly conditioned and ready for anything. Coming from every state and quarter in the U.S., our unit of 140 men reflected almost every possible racial, ethnic, and linguistic diversity we have to offer. More aggressive than ordinary units, the 101st was ready for anything, and we were on the tip of that spear, just where we wanted to be.

In World War II, the Germans surrounded the 101st at Bastogne during the Battle of the Bulge. The 101st held out and was later relieved by Patton's Third Army, but the stand of the unit was legendary. One airborne trooper, on finding out that he was surrounded along with the rest of the 101st, when asked what he thought about his plight, simply said, "Well, the poor bastards have us surrounded."

Right away, I joined in the intensive training that the division had been undergoing for some time. Some soldiers had been through lots of training already, but I found that the rigors I had instituted in Germany were paying off for me in terms of knowledge and how to handle a larger group of men. The hardest exercises were in night fighting. When you can't see and it is difficult to communicate, training becomes a nightmare. Nevertheless, it was deadly serious business, and everyone was attentive, to say the least.

We were warned by veterans of Vietnam that much of the fighting there would be at night—a warning that would prove to be accurate. Every man took the training activity as necessary for survival and wanted to learn every detail and scrap of knowledge the veterans would share. These men had lots of the small tactical nuances that were invaluable. Lessons they had learned the hard way, and we were the beneficiaries. We all wanted to know every trick of the trade to increase our chances of coming home alive.

CHAPTER 2

THE FACE OF THE MOON

We landed at Bien Hoa, Republic of South Vietnam, on a sleek, businesslike commercial Boeing 707. It was a hot, bright, cloudless day in April 1967. The thought that we would storm ashore in a hail of gunfire, like World War II marines in the Pacific, was a fleeting one; instead, our 707 landing was routine, smooth, and uneventful, like the thousands before it. On the long boring flight across the Pacific, pretty stewardesses had served all the sodas and sandwiches with which we could stuff ourselves. Their humor and graciousness were betrayed by the faint sad look in their eyes. They put the best face on what they were doing, and they knew what we were trying in vain to avoid thinking about. Many of the young men they were serving refreshments and make-believe cheer to would die or be shot to pieces in the months ahead.

We were the advance party for our battalion and had much work to do in preparation for the arrival of the rest of the unit. We would have less than two weeks before the battalion arrived. The normal confusion of war greeted us at Bien Hoa, a giant, sprawling supply base and airfield just north of Saigon. Supplies being moved here and there, people rushing about, sergeants screaming to get things done. A lot of hustle and bustle and dust, heat, and sandbags all over the place.

A guide met us, and we boarded a helicopter to fly to an American base called Cu Chi, about thirty miles northwest of Saigon, where we would be based initially. We waited for the remainder of the battalion and started preparing to receive them. Part of our mission was to get ourselves acclimated, both to the environment and to conditions we would meet in the field. This meant gleaning what we could about the realities of combat operations from units in and near Cu Chi and setting up briefings for the day the battalion arrived. Peacetime training was one thing, but as we all knew, actual conditions in the field would be much different, and we had to be prepared.

On the way, we flew over the infamous Iron Triangle, a place I soon would know well. As we flew at a fairly low altitude, I was astonished at the scene below. The countryside had been transformed into a veritable moonscape. So many craters—made by thousands of American bombs and artillery shells—a scant few trees remained. Odd that in an area where verdant, lush growth is the law of nature, there was a moonscape instead. I had never seen anything like it. The moonscape we had created was puzzling. "It's plain goddamn stupid. Why not simply let me and my guys go down there and deal with these commies?" Bombing indiscriminately and on such a massive scale did not seem to be the American way to win a war, and it certainly was not what I expected. We expected to fight on terms that we knew were not equal, but that was all right by us. Paratroops never fought on equal terms, and we would be no different than our older brothers at Bastogne. We were full of swagger, and we were cocky. I wanted to fight, and so did those around me. We were anxious to get at the enemies of the U.S. We would win where the other American combat units before us had not. We knew we would.

As we flew over the Iron Triangle, the heat from the ground reached up and embraced us. In spite of the helicopter's speed and the air rushing through the open helicopter doors, we all had damp fatigues from sweat. Little did we know then that this was a mere sample of what lay ahead and that we would literally sweat for the next dozen or more months.

There was a faint unpleasant smell in the air, not heat alone, but something slightly sinister. Sickly sweet with diesel fuel tones and a bit of stench, the smell crept into the nasal passages. Older hands in Cu Chi said it was latrines, rotting body bits of Vietcong killed by B-52 strikes, or just fetid jungle. A somewhat more prescient or weary person offered that it was simply the smell of Asia. Yet a third sage offered the opinion that it was sewage or night soil, which was collected from countless small villages and hamlets in buckets and literally spread on the fields at night. Close to nature, these people had no other choice for sanitation. It enriched the fields and protected their living areas from disease. A simple but effective system.

As we neared the large American base outside the small Vietnamese village of Cu Chi, one could see vertical pillars of smoke rising from where sewage was being burned in barrels by fuel oil. Since there was no sewer system there either and a high water table during the monsoon, this was a measure of sanitation all American units took. We did not spread our sewage in the fields.

Even flying into this one area, it was clear that the U.S. was taking over the country. Our presence was huge, enormous. I thought, *This is going to be an American war.* So what if that is the case? I'd already heard that the South Vietnamese were useless, and it was fine with me if we did the fighting.

My senses were almost saturated by what I saw: these mere hints of the future, the giant American presence, the incredible force we could use, the simplicity of getting the job done.

Nevertheless, we were green and needed some serious seasoning before there was combat for our group. It was strange that we had flown in comfort to a battlefield and were being shown to relatively comfortable quarters. I had pictured us living in the field and off the land, meeting the enemy on his terms and defeating him there.

From these initial impressions, small doubts began to germinate in my mind. These were the first early indications that something was not quite like I had expected or thought it would be. Some things were quite out of place. Little gray clouds appeared on my once-clear-cut horizon of patriotic black and white. It would take time to discover just how dreadfully wrong things were going. It would take time, patience, and blood to find out just what this cruel war was all about.

When we landed at the Cu Chi airfield, got into jeeps, and headed for our fairly comfortable quarters, my first impression was of the heat. The heat was oppressively overwhelming, and the ample perspiration caused everything to stick to your skin. Paper, sand, and dirt all stuck like it had adhesive. The heat and humidity took your breath away, and I now knew why we had to get acclimated. Had we gone straight into combat, the results could have been disastrous just from the environment, never mind the enemy.

I took a stroll around part of the perimeter and saw bunkers every twenty to thirty feet, and the overall perimeter seemed to be about five miles around. Surprisingly, there were more pockmarked craters scarring the land just outside the perimeter. There were more bunkers, firing positions, and sandbags as I continued my orbit around Cu Chi base. I located our battalion headquarters bunker and went inside. There was the peculiar smell of military canvas—distinct and heavy like the material itself. We used a lot of canvas. It is ubiquitous in the army, and it kept out the dust, rain, and sun.

We had been led to believe in briefings and classes and even in the *Stars and Stripes* that the South Vietnamese Army was a good army, loyal and with the support of the people. An army facing external aggression, an army that only needed a little help from the Americans to counterbalance what the communists were getting from the Soviet Union and Red China. Supporting this army was an implied mission for us.

Cu Chi was a giant base located near the Western approaches to Saigon. To me it seemed a little unusual to see evidence of what seemed to be heavy fighting so close to Saigon. If the South Vietnamese Army was as competent and capable as we had been told and the war against the communists was going as well as our briefings led us to believe, why couldn't the South Vietnamese (and the U.S. Army) even secure the immediate capital area? How did the communists get so close? Before leaving Fort Campbell, Kentucky, where the 101st Airborne Division had been stationed, we heard rumors about the low ability of South Vietnamese units. Briefings said otherwise, but facts on the ground speak for themselves.

Why were we being stationed here anyway? We all wanted to be dropped as airborne troops in the region between Haiphong and Hanoi to "wring the chicken's neck, not pluck its feathers," as I once said back in the U.S. Many of us genuinely felt we were being sent to the wrong place. After a lot of soldiers asked me this and similar questions, it made me start thinking about those people in the Joint Chiefs of Staff in the Pentagon. What information were they using to make such decisions? Who was calling the shots in this war, and what was the goal of the war? It seemed that we had little direction or guidance, except tactical fighting.

I began to hear a voice in my head saying, *Beware, this is a land where things may not be as they seem or as we have been told.* Be on guard; be alert. My sensory antennae were fully arrayed. "Something is wrong, something is out of place."

Second impressions were more routine, and after a day or two of talking to troops and officers who had been in-country longer, I gradually formed a clearer picture of what was going on in this war. I was wary, even though most veteran soldiers tried to impress us with their combat experience and knowledge. Many of the officers seemed intent on trying to outdo one another in scaring us, a foolish tactic, I thought, of an amateur.

One of the most startling revelations of my new experience then hit me. Walking down one of Cu Chi's dusty roads, I came up to the PX. This was a large post exchange (PX) or shopping center. At this store, many of the allied troops, especially Thai troops, could be seen attacking this facility with vigor, carrying off all sorts of American-made goodies. They would start lining up an hour before the PX opened and stay in the store for hours. Signs of creature comforts at Cu Chi were obvious almost everywhere. What really started to sink in for me was the fact that none of these men wanted to fight! They were all seeking ways to stay out of the jungle, or the bush as we called it. They did not have the combative spirit of the airborne; they simply wanted to do their time and get out. This was especially true of our allies, but many an American soldier also fell into this category. The sheer number of men involved in the supporting, manning, and administrative activities for such stores was enormous. Each man here was one less in an infantry unit.

What I had seen of Bien Hoa and then Cu Chi told me that many troops—countless tens of thousands—were occupied in logistics, headquarters, and various support roles. Officers were more concerned over their hooch (living quarters) than anything else. Enlisted men seemed to be always on mindless errands, just doing nothing. Few soldiers, it appeared, were anxious to fight the enemy, and no one seemed to know anything about the general tactical situation. I thought I had a strange war on my hands.

After the shock of the PX, one more jolt was in store for me. As I continued my tour of Cu Chi, I spotted white-painted rocks lining the driveways in the headquarters area. This was the ultimate sign of garrison life back in the U.S. Garrison life at an army base in peacetime developed its own routine and became a military city, complete with everything you would find in a small town in the U.S., the difference being that it was all military.

I thought painted rocks and that sort of thing had been done away with during the period between the two World Wars, but there they were in living color. There were more of these cute markers near the base commander's living quarters, and even the driveway between them was lined with rocks painted white! One could traverse Cu Chi and not see a weapon. One soldier told me he was doing the exact same thing he had been doing in the Pentagon, only now he was stationed in Vietnam. It appeared that the logistics tail was huge, and the teeth of the army were not that sharp. To me, painting rocks white were the ultimate sign of wasted effort and meaningless work.

In South Asia, there were huge bases, not just in Vietnam, but in Thailand for the air force and numerous ships at sea. The U.S. had an enormous, indeed incredible support structure built to take care of an incredibly large army. But there were far too many soldiers avoiding fighting and engaged in all kinds of garrison life. Avoiding the hazards of the infantry seemed a passion to many. One we in the airborne could not understand. These people were soldiers, and they had a bad attitude. Even as an officer new to Vietnam, I knew this meant there would be too few soldiers in combat units or equally bad, simply too-few combat units.

There were several American divisions in Vietnam now: the First Air Cav, the Twenty-Fifth Infantry, Fourth Infantry, and, of course, the marines. We had heard that the Fourth Infantry had a poor combat record, and morale was low. We also knew that the enemy looked for this division, feeling it was easier prey. Rear area troops seemed to have no morale and only wanted creature comforts while some combat troops we saw were simply resigned to their fate. By contrast, our attitude was still "Let's go get 'em."

This mental processing of mine was quickly and brutally interrupted by men in the dark, the Vietcong, wearing what looked like pajamas, who illustrated vividly just why the scars of battle were so close. They did not shirk from their duty; they came right at us in a brief but serious clash. One of the first nameless little skirmishes that would make no difference in the war but would kill men.

After a few days in-country, several beautiful young Vietnamese women in the traditional Vietnamese dress called *ao dai*s brought us flowers to welcome our unit and to express thanks for our help to their country. Two nights later, some of the same women were killed when they tried to fight their way through the perimeter of barbed-wire fences, bunkers, mines, fougasse barrels, and fields of fire, which surrounded Cu Chi. Slight and small, the women carried light bangalore torpedoes, designed to blow passage ways through barbed wire and mines, so that their men could follow through with greater ease and get inside our position where they could wreak the most damage. While this was not a major attack or even one that could cause any real damage, it was an indicator.

This incident, which had taken place on the opposite side of the base from where we were, left a profound impression. All kinds of images and thoughts were making circuit rides through my mind. As a novice at war and only briefly in Vietnam, I felt judgments were probably wrong or at least premature. But as a Southerner, the oral history of my past was starting to set off alarm bells about lost causes and despair. Way back, in the part of your mind where you store little but conscience and character, a voice started to whisper, saying things like, "What in the hell are we doing?" "Is this woefully wrong or just a reflection of my skewered, newcomer outlook?"

"Why are local civilians who are supposed to be our allies trying to kill us?" "Are we fighting the war incorrectly, or is it an unjust war or what?" "Are the protesters right?" There was little comfort in these early impressions. American casualty lists were growing, and I knew we were in for a lot of fighting. Most troubling of all was the frightening thought that my intuition—the quiet whispers—might just be right.

A day later, it was time for action, the first patrol. Now we would meet the enemy. We would kick his collective commie ass and get the war won. Airborne troops don't give up easily. About twenty-five of us moved out of the Cu Chi perimeter at first sunlight on a familiarization patrol. We were led by a couple of seasoned veterans and assured that the area we were headed for was safe, and contact with the enemy was only the remotest of possibilities. We were being familiarized with patrol techniques, vegetation, how to move, etc., all good stuff we needed to know. Our uniforms were hot as the sun blistered down. Wet spots appeared almost instantly, and as the day wore on, it was easy to discover why no one ever wore underwear in the field. You were almost always wet with sweat in the humidity and rain of South Asia. Too much moisture could cause crotch rot and other unpleasant side effects.

Our load, the load of the infantry, added to the discomfort. The ammunition tugged heavily, and the two canteens full of water, first-aid pouch, rations for the day, entrenching tool, flak jacket, web gear, steel helmet, at least two hand grenades, a smoke grenade or two, and a gas mask and personal items all pulled at your body. When you were out for longer periods, you had to take more food and ammunition and a poncho to sleep on. You felt like you could not catch your breath, and as you walked, you gasped for air, but it felt almost like you were not getting any. The straps of your web gear, which held the weight of your gear, cut into your shoulders, leaving a furrow and sometimes permanent scars. Our load was usually sixty to seventy pounds, a lot for the conditions we were under.

To this heavy load, the young men of America would have to add another. One far more difficult than a few belts of machine gun ammunition or another canteen. No, this would not weigh an ounce, but it would be one of the heaviest burdens ever carried by an American soldier—the psychological one.

We'd gone a few miles and come up on a low sandy ridge that did not have much tree growth. You could see quite a way, across some rice paddies and open clear fields. As we moved our twenty-five-man patrol up and across this ridge, I thought of taking a break. I had never really thought about the need to relieve oneself during combat. In training, we had pee breaks, but it didn't seem to relate to war itself. About then, I heard some loud bees or hornets buzzing around and said to the first sergeant, "Jesus, what kind of bugs are these?" He looked at me with just a faint hint of a smile (possibly a bit of contempt) and said, "Well, Captain, back in Korea, we used to call 'em bullets."

I was thunderstruck. Someone was shooting at us, at me, and I didn't even know it, much less where the fire was coming from or even what to do about it. Instinctively, I yelled, "Hit the dirt!" and we all did with the flair of novices. Gathering my wits, I directed rifle and machine gun fire toward the area we thought the enemy fire had originated. The firing stopped, and we moved out to "close with, and kill or capture the enemy"—according to the infantry manual. In case the enemy had fled, I told everyone to look for spent shell casings so we could identify the weapons and enemy location and report it to the intelligence people. We did not find any empty brass shell casings, but we did find where the enemy had been positioned and fired at us.

What kind of people were we fighting? Who picked up their spent shells? Whoever heard of such a thing in war? Did they reload the shells, or was it just to deny us any information about their weapons? Who were these people? I wanted to know more about them and why they were fighting in such a peculiar manner.

We rested for a few moments, ate our C ration lunches, reorganized our patrol, and continued our journey. The rest of the patrol was uneventful, hot and tiring, but no further excitement. When we got back in to Cu Chi just before dark, I filled out a combat report. We had no casualties, not a shred of intelligence on the enemy, nothing, just a mundane, silly report about nothing. Would anyone at division or corps headquarters glean anything from it? I had the feeling there would be lots of reports like this.

I reflected back on my little hometown and humble background. Now everything was different, changed in perceptible, tangible ways. I was in charge and would soon be commanding over a hundred sons of America. The rest of the battalion would be here in days, and we would start operating as a unit and no doubt be in heavy fighting. I liked the trust that they gave me, and I was determined to repay the U.S. for the honor of being made an officer and a leader. We had a war to win, and we were going to do just that. I couldn't sleep that night, thinking about what lay ahead. I was excited and anxious about what would our year be like and how would we all end up.

I had come in from my first patrol, and I had not done too badly.

CHAPTER 3

MEN DIE HARD

The cutting edge is sharper for the infantry than any other fighting or noncombat units. There is always more blood because the enemy who seeks us and the enemy whom we seek usually meet up in combat. It is a hard fact of life as a soldier, but we knew this was our lot, and what it meant.

The battalion had arrived and had gone through some limited training, and we were expected to initiate combat operations in a day or so. We were now about to venture into the "Valley of the Shadow of Death." As the inscription on one airborne soldier's shirt said, "I'm in the valley of the shadow of death and I fear no one because I'm the meanest son of a bitch in the valley." Good spirit for the airborne.

When I had arrived at Fort Campbell, Kentucky, from Germany some long months before, I had seen the division commander and volunteered for the reconnaissance company, which was known as the hardest fighting element in the division. This would be the unit that was first into an area and last out. We would have specially trained troops, airborne, rangers, special forces, and engineers—our special skills would be in high demand. Now I was starting to wonder if I was the victim of my own poor judgment.

In a blur of activity, we moved to Dau Tieng, way out west of Saigon, close to the border with Cambodia, in the middle of War Zone C. War zones were designated as C or D. Perhaps there were others, an A and B, but I was unaware of them.

The war zones were supposedly void of any friendly Vietnamese. They had all been moved to government resettlement camps (a euphemism for new slums and slum dwellers in Saigon). Population normally had been sparse in the war zones, and the jungle was dense and supreme. This is where the famous triple canopy (three layers of vegetation) was.

U.S. military forces were allowed to treat anyone in a war zone as hostile, and the war zones were considered free fire zones, in that we did not have to preclear (obtain permission to fire) artillery fires, air strikes, and the like. We could engage without clearances from anyone.

Units could operate with near abandon. Still, the zones were also near the Ho Chi Minh trail, and the enemy could be very dangerous there since he would fight hard to protect his meager supply lines. Enemy troops could also move very quickly to attack us and disappear just as fast. To most of us, the war zones were more dangerous for us than the enemy, and the zones usually meant heavy fighting.

We were billeted next to the giant French-owned Michelin rubber plantation, known to all grunts (riflemen) as the rubber. Dau Tieng, also called Tri Tam, was the name of the nearby Vietnamese village. Our camp had numerous run-down French buildings, some of which had been quite nice at one time but by now were spartan. The French plantation had once been a vibrant enterprise but now was dilapidated and very down at the heels, in that it gave the impression of being poor. Knowing what happened to the French military in Vietnam, with their disastrous series of defeats and setbacks culminating at Dien Bien Phu, gave us cold comfort. The French had fought well and, in the end, had been compelled by Ho Chi Mihn to surrender and leave Vietnam. Well, we had only the southern half of Vietnam to worry about and a lot more support and ability than the French. No worry.

The rubber was a dangerous place. The trees were all planted in rows, and there was a good interconnecting road system all the way up to the Cambodian border. This place scared the hell out of me because I knew how fast Vietcong troops could be moved against us. Stonewall Jackson could move his Confederate infantry twenty-five miles in a day and be ready to fight when he got to his destination. We could be facing a huge enemy force with little or no warning, night or day, but that's why we were there—to fight. That is the mission of the infantry. Our attitudes began to transform overnight to the thoughts of what we would soon be facing.

The battalion commander was visibly worried since intelligence had told him there may be an entire regiment or two operating in the area. An enemy regiment could have 2,500 men. That particular day, we numbered almost 900 men. All four of my platoon leaders and their key NCOs were also on edge, especially in view of the fact that we would probably not be able to call on our friends—air strikes and artillery—if we got in trouble. We all knew if a regiment or two hit us, it would probably mean we would be overrun and annihilated.

Our initial actions took place around a small village in the rubber called Ap Bis 13, which consisted of nothing more than a few grass huts with wood frames, some with wooden floors, some with no more than a dirt floor. None had plumbing or lights. These were simple peasant huts, and the people eked out a subsistence life. A few pieces of rusty, worn-out French equipment for harvesting and processing the latex sap of the rubber trees littered the area. Ap Bis 13 would have made an excellent photo page in National Geographic.

When an infantry unit moves out on an operation, a lot of planning has to be accomplished. The mission has to be explained (briefed) to all company commanders, lieutenants, and sergeants. These men then explain the objective and mission to the soldiers who will do most of the fighting. Maps need to be distributed and briefed. Artillery has to be in range and ready to fire if called on. Artillery units liked to register their guns by firing them to establish better accuracy. The forward observer has to be aware of what artillery units will be in range and what type of fire will be available if needed. The air force has to be on standby, and both forms of fire support must be able to communicate over the radio, which means a common frequency and good communications all around. Resupply flights, especially for ammunition, and potential medevac flights have to be planned. If other American units are nearby, there must be coordination with them to reduce the possibility of friendly fire. Weapons have to be checked and rechecked, uniforms replaced if needed, and anything badly worn replaced. Each man must prepare himself with adequate ammunition, food, and water and anything else he is responsible for. My radioman always had to carry at least two extra batteries for the radio. This was no small thing as the batteries weighed a couple of pounds and were about half the size of a loaf of bread. We changed the radio battery at least once a day to make sure we always had good power.

When all of this preparation is complete, an infantry unit is basically ready to move out and fight if it has to. I must also say that a large part is psychological, and when coupled with the bonding that men do in such instances, it all helps motivate one to do what must be done.

However, an infantry unit can use several formations as it moves through open terrain, woods, fields, or whatever situation may present itself. In most formations, there is what is known as the point man. Without any doubt, this is the most hazardous job in the infantry. The point man is the first man out, the first to see the enemy or be seen by him. He is frequently the first to find a booby-trapped area or a minefield. The courage it takes to walk point is tremendous; the stress is simply incredible. No medal can reward the infantryman who quietly takes his turn as the point man for a unit. He is truly in "the valley of the shadow of death." Others also take great risk, forward observers, platoon leaders, anyone carrying a radio, and so on, but it takes special moral and physical courage to walk point.

As our point man and the rest of the company moved close to Ap Bis 13 and the other companies of the battalion followed, firing broke out. Two companies, one of them mine, quickly moved around the village and assaulted it from two sides. We moved cautiously into the village; there was not a single enemy soldier around any longer. There was no evidence of their firing even though my point man was badly hit and lay dying with two bullets from an AK-47 in his chest. Actually, one bullet had ripped through his upper chest at an ugly angle, leaving bone and tissue hanging out of the top of his shoulder. The other bullet had taken a mysterious path, and we saw no exit point.

Death in war is far more brutal and hideous than I imagined; even a careful reader of such events would have to be shocked at the absolute horror of seeing a young man literally torn apart. In fact, war movies come off as nearly silly in the light touch they give to such events. It is not romantic or patriotic. Hurt men do not cry softly or dictate letters to loved ones back home. In the violent carnage of war, men are dismembered, arms blown off, stomachs ripped open, faces shot off, hips torn asunder, lungs exposed. The badly wounded scream with an intensity unlike anything else and thrash violently. Blood flies, and they convulse in agony. Even light wounds bring a soldier down; the body simply obeys nature. Some men are simply blown to pieces—dismembered and dead before they can even react.

Slowly, breath by breath, the life escaped from this young American in a place called Ap Bis 13, far from home, far from anything relevant to him, his family or even his country. It was a pointless little engagement, not in the evening news or even the official military communiqués. It would barely be mentioned in our battalion log, just an incident, one soon forgotten. The death of a soldier would have been acceptable if on the whole we were doing something worthwhile. But we were all starting to question what our combined sacrifices would accomplish. I followed his body once we were back in Dau Tieng. It was enclosed in a green plastic body bag with a tag attached for identification. Soon the remains would be refrigerated and sent to the U.S. for burial. Vibrant, capable young men, the sons of America, were arriving in Vietnam, and body bags were being sent home.

The villagers of Ap Bis 13 were questioned by South Vietnamese Army interpreters. Of course, not a single one knew a thing, and they all swore the firing came from somewhere else. The battalion commander decided they must be evacuated to a government resettlement camp. As soon as the helicopters arrived and forty to fifty people were taken out, we burned the village to the ground. It was the first time I heard the phrase, "Let's burn it down to save 'em." This also was my first interaction with the South Vietnamese Army, and the impression was not favorable in the least. Could these be the same people who seemed to be such capable adversaries? One soldier called the Vietnamese "our kittens and the VC were lions." Our Vietnamese were slovenly, had no pretense of being soldiers, and were clearly despised by the people they interacted with. They treated the villagers with brutal indifference, shooting in the air, kicking children, and so forth. They carried commercial radios for music, had a crazy mixture of useless stuff around, and were, by our accounts, more like a gang than soldiers.

From this small incident, it seemed a highly misguided policy to uproot agricultural people, send them to a resettlement camp, burn their humble homes, and then hope to win their hearts and minds. This was not doing anything for the goals of the U.S. or even more directly for us. It just appeared stupid and destructive. We were making enemies of the people we had supposedly come to assist. I could only imagine how many Vietcong our little action had created. We had come in, done much damage, and departed. Sons coming back to such a scene would be eager recruits for the Vietcong.

The soldiers in the American Army knew this by intuition and by what they say. Young officers knew the same thing, but our feelings and thoughts never penetrated past Saigon, where legions of staff officers and toadies coated everything with sugar. All was well. We were winning the war, and they had statistics to prove it all.

The poor people we had uprooted were wedded to the land. Without their land, they would become slum dwellers in Saigon or worse. They knew nothing but the land and farming. On their land, they could sustain themselves and their children, and it was their ancestral heritage. What we were taking part in was cruel and unwarranted, a fact driven home by screaming children and parents being physically forced on to helicopters, some with their hands tied. We began to hear that the resettlement camps were little more than nightmares, something the villagers already knew.

We simply did what we were told and kept within the confines of the rules of war. We did not commit any atrocities or do evil deeds, but no one liked this mission. We all thought it was odious and smelled bad. Too bad a U.S. senator was not here with us watching. We would have even settled for a senate staffer or anyone from Washington. Arrogance takes many forms, and we were witness to one.

CHAPTER 4

DIMINUTIVE MEN, LION-SIZED HEARTS

After the first few violent contacts or firefights, I began to wonder who were those small men who died so readily. Their courage was reckless. It caused one to try to imagine what it must have been like from their side, facing the incredible U.S. killing machine. Our firepower was overwhelmingly awesome. We had a wealth of artillery few armies could ever dream of and our incredible airpower, which must have been unbelievable to them. With our multiple communications networks, we could bring these to bear on the enemy within moments. Even the lowly infantrymen had mountains of ammunition and more machine guns, mortars, grenades, and direct-fire weapons than we could efficiently manage.

Yet they kept coming, inflicting as much pain on us as possible, expending themselves dearly when possible. Who sent those small men who fought like lions? The mothers of North Vietnam must have known the price they were paying was a river of tears. One could only imagine a farewell in Hanoi. Many were heading south; none were coming back. We were slaughtering an entire generation.

Uncertainty prevailed again. The numbers of enemy troops we were killing effectively shattered their units (by our standards) and should have decided the fighting. We had cleared entire provinces, and they should have stayed that way. However, each time we returned to such an area, we knew it had not been secured but only temporarily made safe by our presence. Enemy casualties were astronomical. The South should be winning the war and pushing up to the border with the North. The way the enemy was losing, it seemed like they should sue for peace any day, but . . .

The enemy knew what they were fighting for, and their society was perfectly willing to make the sacrifices necessary to achieve what they thought was right. They had a cause; they had a crusade. They were fighting for their homes, farms, families, and unity of their country. While we knew their propaganda was excellent, much of what we observed went deeper than that. There was a distinct lack of the hollow ring of untruth. They were fanatical about this war and willing to go the distance, no matter how far that may be.

We had nothing comparable against the Vietnamese; they were not going to invade the U.S. nor could they do us any real harm. While most of us understood that we were fighting communism (the Soviet Union by proxy), this was not evident on the battlefield. We were the outsiders, the foreigners who threatened their homes, their way of life. **We** were the invaders. As far as the Vietnamese peasants were concerned, we could have been from Mars or some other planet. We were that alien to them.

In the rice paddies and forests, as the days blurred with a monotonous familiarity, we read of home and the events taking place there. Home, the sanctuary of our minds and sanity. Home took on the reverence most have for mother, and U.S. soldiers in Vietnam used it synonymously. Most of us felt, at that stage, that we could do this. We could hang on in the Nam if there was home.

Helicopters came in to our positions each evening to bring supplies, ammunition above all, and we often got copies of the *Stars and Stripes*, printed for troops in Vietnam and elsewhere in the region. Mail had some priority, and we got our mail from home, along with the newspapers from the States. We read more and more about the street riots and demonstrations against the war and the soul-searching America was going through. New replacements told us how much we were hated and despised by those who had sent us. We knew now that we were now being called baby killers.

To men drafted to fight a war they were not really committed to or prepared for, morale sagged, which caused many units to perform at a lower level, which in turn caused more casualties. Caught in a deadly and vicious cycle, we were becoming more isolated than ever. A type of mental confusion was growing and spreading, and no level of rank or experience could immunize one from catching it.

The gnawing whisper of just a few weeks before was indeed turning up in volume. A hint in my mind was now an avalanche of warnings. The warning flags were up. We were in trouble, serious trouble. I started using the word "quagmire" more often and found it to be a perfect fit. Soldiers understood the meaning and agreed with it. We felt little or no pressure from above to be different. Most of our above was at the battalion level, and while we all wanted to do well and win the war, politics was just not our game at this point.

I desperately wanted to stop the communists in Vietnam. I was a soldier and knew that there would be killing and hardships, but I did not avoid entering into such an arena. I wanted to grind their military into the ground and then let the politicians do whatever they needed to do. I knew the communists were wrong and not too much different from the Nazis. But it was becoming clear that this was a civil war, and *their* side had far better leaders than those in the South, and they were motivated by a cause. Our side—South Vietnam—was empty; there was nothing but corruption and decadence.

The United States was allied with Saigon and all that South Vietnam did not stand for. The North had clearly taken the international propaganda or press lead. They were exploiting the left liberal causes and playing on what appeared to be common sense around the world. Hanoi, supported by Moscow, had seized the propaganda high ground and would retain it. Hanoi was looking ahead at each step; Saigon was making deposits in its Swiss bank accounts.

The way we were attempting to stop the communists defied logic. One could only think that the methods being employed in Vietnam, not just in combat, but across the board, had been devised by people who did not have the slightest idea of the conditions and overall situation in that country. Who was thinking of this at our huge headquarters in Saigon? Soldiers thought we were doing more damage than good. For every VC we killed, probably two more joined up. Their observations appeared to be correct. For the first time, the thought that we would lose the war crossed my thoughts fleetingly. I purged it as impossible from my mind. The U.S. could not lose a war against a small backwater country, could it?

Meanwhile, the fighting went on. What resonated inside me was the nightmarish quality of the whirlwind around us and the frailty of life. I was in a helicopter one early morning when we received ground fire. The copilot was wounded just below the knee by an AK-47 bullet fired by an unseen enemy. Our helicopter quickly flew back to Dau Tieng, and the copilot was sent to the hospital in Cu Chi, and even though his wound was not thought to be life threatening, he died the same day. Other soldiers who had been much more seriously wounded recovered. It seemed like a giant game of craps. Sometimes you were lucky, and sometimes you were not.

There were no great offensives, no major objectives to be taken in this war. But to the individual soldier, every day was D-day. You could delude yourself, and when you felt like you were on a mere stroll in the woods, the sharp crack of a rifle would reintroduce reality. Even at this stage, we could see no end to it, just a daily, weekly affair of little overall consequence. Random death, such as that caused by a booby trap or an unseen sniper, all worked to psychologically isolate us and forced us to realize that the war, after all, was not orderly and not really important, except to us. It left us with a strange and distant feeling.

We read and heard of the bacchanalian home front of Woodstock, free love, war protest songs, and of Johnson's guns and butter ideas. These were conflicting concepts and ideas even to us. But we soldiers were the only ones making sacrifices in a war we were told was important but was not. We were fighting, but not the Red Army in Europe, and we were not protecting our homes, families, democracy, or anything. Consumer spending was up. Life was going on in the U.S., and the war was a sideshow, and we knew it. Guys grumbled every day about what was going on back home, some just to one another, some just to themselves, but it was a deep wound in our minds.

It seemed to us that few people cared, except perhaps our immediate families. The war had been presented in such a way that few people *could care*. We knew that even those responsible for the war knew us as numbers and had their own body count of U.S. troops. We were just statistics to them, not our boys as President Roosevelt said countless times in World War II. All of this made a difference.

CHAPTER 5

WHO IS CHARLIE?

Our enemy at this point in the war was the Vietcong, who had a reputation as elusive, tough, and enigmatic. "Charlie will cut your balls off." First words I ever heard about him. It did not seem too clear to us as to why Charlie would even fight; it seemed so illogical and counterintuitive. Clearly, we were right and going to win. Evidence and intelligence told a lot about the enemy, except what were they fighting for, and why were they able to hold us at bay. Troubling questions for us. Our world, the combat elements of the army, was quite simply black and white. This element of confusion was most unwelcome. The fact that Charlie was fighting for his ideas and his way of life in effect for his own independence seemed ludicrous to us.

In the military, the alphabet was reduced to phonetic words—Alpha, Beta, Charlie, Delta, and so on—ostensibly to help understand when radio communications were bad and to make messages shorter and uniform so everyone could understand them. The name Vietcong was shortened to VC, and in the military alphabet, he became Victor Charlie. Well, no one liked the victor part, so his name was shortened to Charlie, an almost friendly term with none of the hate-filled resonance of Krauts or Japs. Another of the small ideological elements that helped cripple the American war aims and effort, at least in the minds of U.S. combat soldiers.

We needed some of the tough edge of war. Killing is a dirty, hideous affair, and the stage has to be set for it. If we are going to make that kind of commitment—the decision to go to war—it should be with our entire materiel and psychological arsenal. Indeed, the entire fabric of American society has to be engaged to be successful. The U.S., for all its skill in marketing, had failed miserably to market the war to the American people, including its soldiers, and now they were not buying the domino theory or any other crap coming out of Washington or our higher headquarters.

The home front was even less willing to buy this, and it showed. As an officer, I almost dreaded mail call because I knew it would contain newspapers with the darkest slant on what was being done in Vietnam. Mail is supposed to be a brief, wonderful relief, but many a well-meaning person back home put in comments or thoughts that were devastating to men in this war. Some men held it in; others did show it and became more troublesome. One man, upon getting a letter from his young wife saying she was leaving him, promptly charged into withering enemy machine gun fire and solved his problem in a manner undoubtedly taken by many soldiers though the centuries. To be fair, though, most letters from home were what one would expect—full of love and concern—and they were precious indeed to all of us.

They were small men, the Vietnamese, usually only five feet or so. One big captain (about six feet eight) in our battalion could hold out his arm, grab a small tree, and let our Vietnamese interpreters do pull-ups on his arm. Great fun. We were big, well off in military terms, endowed with more equipment than the Vietcong could dream of, and yet . . .

Our enemy was poor, with no aircraft, no artillery (except mortars), and little in the way of communications. We had an abundance of everything. He was not physically as strong as the large Americans, and he was also hungry when we were full. We knew this since we sometimes doubled back to our former positions and would find all our garbage pits, where we threw unused C rations, had been dug up, and any salvageable rations had been devoured on the spot. It did not seem to matter that he was no better, not even as good as we were at fighting in the bush or elsewhere. The little shits were good.

Charlie had a cause. He was eager for combat. He would close in on our units to fight us as close as possible in order to void our artillery and air power. This took careful control by enemy officers since mistakes would, and did, expose Charlie to American firepower. He had the one thing we did not have. He wanted to fight. He was defending his home, his family, his way of life, and he would do that until we killed every single enemy soldier in the country. (Of course, that was the problem. Everyone in the country was a soldier or was becoming one.) We had become demonized, and Charlie would die to get us out of his country.

I considered the differences that this psychological imbalance made, and they were enormous. Charlie would fight to the last man. As more weeks went by, this happened several more times as we shattered some of their units. Even battle-hardened infantrymen hesitated to kill those who had fought so hard yet would not surrender. When we had to kill like this, there was no sense of accomplishment or that we had done something good. Charlie maneuvered well, without radios, using only voice commands and common sense.

I had read numerous volumes on the Civil War and the great asymmetries in resources and capabilities between North and South. Charlie reminded me in some small ways of the privations Confederate soldiers must have endured. The Confederates, under their great captain Lee, also fought with flair. It also dawned on me that the Confederates were fighting on their own farms and land as well, even though their cause was a flawed one.

We did not hate Charlie; it would have been easier to fight them if we had. In war, there are always questions concerning fairness and atrocities. Charlie would probably have committed some against us had he had the chance. Only later would I see U.S. troops commit what could perhaps or technically be called an atrocity.

Our battalion had been operating for about two weeks in War Zone D, near a place called Loc Ninh, when we surrounded an enemy unit, a North Vietnamese battalion of some 350-400 men. After two days of long and heavy fighting, they had been ground down by American artillery fire, air strikes, and our infantry weapons. The fighting had all but ended, and the VCs were dead except for two badly wounded survivors. One of the two appeared to be a medic. We had the interpreters request both of them to surrender. Neither enemy soldier replied. Our Vietnamese (we had several attached to our battalion during this operation) and a few U.S. troops went forward to the enemy positions in order to check out the wounded enemy troops. One wounded VC had a pistol but was too badly wounded to actually fire. He tried in vain to aim but was killed instantly. The other tried to bite a medic who attempted to tend his wounds. A distraught, tired infantryman casually blew the last man's head off. It was like shooting a dog with rabies.

This was not the war I signed up to fight. *This was a sickening fucking war, one with no reason or justification, just a war.*

Charlie was tough in ways the uninformed did not understand. A few days after this episode, we heard a story about a group of congressmen who were touring parts (safe areas) of Vietnam. One had seen some Vietcong prisoners and remarked that they were wearing shoes made out of scavenged, cut-up U.S. military tires. The congressman declared that they must be on their last legs economically if they had to steal tires and make shoes out of them. One of my guys said, "Hell, Captain, you can probably get one hundred thousand miles on a pair of those shoes."

In the infantry, we all knew that those tire shoes were probably the best the Vietcong soldiers had ever had. In our superabundance, *we were actually supplying the enemy* with our discarded materiel and assisting in his war effort. Most alarmingly, the representatives of the U.S. Government had taken home exactly the wrong message. As with much of what was going on, they did not ask us about our impressions, but they loudly declared what they thought was true. They had found their facts in carefully staged briefing rooms in Saigon and very limited field tours in controlled, safe areas and would take such crazy impressions home to the public.

At any rate, that was not what the war was about nor was it particularly relevant. But it was a warning about the naïveté of our elected officials who did not understand the true nature of the conflict they had sent us to fight. They clearly did not see a civil war, a social revolution, a society throwing off what it could not tolerate. We were or had become part of the problem. The people who sent us to Vietnam could not understand or see that simple fact. They should have taken the time to ask some simple infantrymen basic questions rather than listening to pabulum briefings in Saigon and being told such contradictory and ridiculous things as there was a "light at the end of the tunnel." One soldier in my company summed it up very well with the succinct comment: "Fucking idiots!"

The soldiers did not like the politicians and the establishment back home that had sent them to this hellhole. Fully aware that the antiestablishment and liberals back home did not like the soldiers, we were caught on the losing end of a three-way tug-of-war. Men grew to feel intense loyalty to one another and their families back home. Everyone else was fair game.

Indeed, most of us thought that the light at the end of the tunnel was a muzzle flash from an AK-47. This bit of personal wisdom was relayed to a reporter from the *Stars and*

Stripes. It ran as a small byline and earned me more than a few disparaging looks and comments from senior officers. I knew that this voice of dissent would not be well received, but I felt a comment like that was innocuous enough, and I did want it to be reported in the press. We knew the press would grab anything that put the war in a negative light.

We Americans were not helping to win Vietnam from the communists. Our confusion was starting to become apparent even in the war effort. Would we build a wall around Vietnam? Would we send in still more troops? Would nuclear weapons be used? I began to wonder if our leaders had a true or could ever get a true picture of what was going on at our level, on the ground in Vietnam. I could not believe that the government could know the true situation and still keep us there to pursue the war in the same fashion, using the same clearly self-defeating mechanisms.

The fashion of this war was to empower a corrupt government and fight for it. Instead of serious land or economic reforms, we were carpet bombing with B-52s and destroying village after village in search and destroy missions. Too few combat troops in the field and far too many noncombat troops in Saigon and Bien Hoa, where stories of corruption, prostitution, smuggling, and drugs were filtering out to us. You don't win a society to a decent cause by turning their daughters into prostitutes.

We had allowed the communists victory on a psychological and economic level where we could clearly have won. The communists had won at the village level. Their men came into villages, especially at night, and the troops of the South did not. We had let the North, and presumably Peking and Moscow, win the propaganda war and, with it, much of the support we could have brought to bear against them. All they had to do was stay engaged and not quit. They could win by dragging out the war as long as they needed to.

Again, I listened to the wisdom of soldiers, who repeatedly said, "Captain, why the hell are we here?"

My answer was usually something like, "I don't know either, but our job is to live through the day." These men were not being insubordinate or churlish. They really did not know why we were there, and they did not believe what they had been told. Especially after they had been in combat and seen some of the things we were doing. It is hard to ask men to risk their lives in this kind of scenario.

CHAPTER 6

THE INSTITUTIONALIZATION OF DEATH

The thunder of artillery was near, always near, and we institutionalized the process of death. I had been some three months in-country, and in addition to the earlier maladies of diarrhea, tremors became a regular occurrence for me after a firefight, even if it was almost nothing, like a few rounds of sniper fire. It did not feel like the trembling when a person gets cold or an unusual fright. It was much deeper. In a way, it was like palsy, but the adrenaline of a fight or intense activity would instantly cure the condition. It was always afterward, when things were quiet, that it was most severe and difficult to control. I guessed it was the war and all the unusual things that were very new; I hoped that the experience of becoming a veteran would enable me to get used to combat, used to what was happening, and train me to control my reactions more effectively. I never consulted a medic or doctors back at a main base like Cu Chi. I knew the answer, and it was wrapped around the fact that I did not want to die for a worthless cause, and it was eating my soul to be part of the process that was sending others to die.

Overhead, the giant B-52 bombers cruised with their tons of bombs. We did not hear these aircraft or see them, but we received special warnings from our headquarters, so we did not venture near where the bombers were going to release their lethal loads of death to glide silently to earth. When the bombs hit—five-hundred-, one-thousand-, and two-thousand-pound versions—the effect was like a thunderous earthquake, even though we were miles away. I thought of those people under the bombs and knew they must have died by the hundreds. There was no protection from one-ton bombs; even good, well-constructed bunkers were turned to dust. Tunnels caved in to become ready-made graves, and even the concussion from the blast would kill those close enough.

We were sometimes ordered to exploit an arc-light target a few hours after a bombing to evaluate the effects of America's industrialized war effort. "Arc-light" was the code name the military gave to the B-52 strikes. It probably had no specific meaning. The first time my company went in to do a damage assessment was revealing. As I was stepping off a helicopter, the first thing I saw was a hand on the ground, neatly severed at the wrist. Nearby was the distinctive tip end of a Russian AK-47 assault rifle, also neatly severed, almost like a hacksaw had cut it off. It was awesome, gruesome, and sickening. There was death everywhere. Our immediate concern was to live through the day, to make yourself as comfortable as possible, and hope your number did not come up, hope the body bags were not for you. So we would do as ordered, carry out an exploitation, and move on.

We were going about that business, that war, in an orderly fashion, almost mechanical, as though we were on autopilot. The meager resources of Vietnam, such as timber, were being devastated. How could we hope to win these people over to our side when we were not representing democracy or the Western world as we should have been allowed to, had those in high places in Washington done their work more effectively.

While we were good at the military aspects of what we were doing, there was no soul, no purpose to it. Our technology was supreme, but we were fighting against an idea, a concept, and that underlying cause gave our foe his one great advantage.

We did not have that elusive spirit that one empowered by ideas has. We were doing **what** we were told to do, but the confusion in Washington made us gradually realize that the mission we were on was a lie. Politicians probably do not realize just how hard it is to fool a soldier out there, walking point or involved in serious combat; troops can tell the difference between bullshit and truth. Out in Asia, far removed from Washington's inner workings, reality is stark, truth is blunt, infantrymen can see through the lies of soft-handed men. Anger at our situation and a desperate desire to stay alive gripped us all. We felt helpless. Imagine that, men armed to the teeth but helpless in the face of a cruel war and events taking place around us.

The question of why nations went to war caused me to think about our situation over and over in a vain attempt to rationalize what was happening and why I was fighting. What was important enough to compel entire societies to take this fateful and dangerous step? The U.S., during the '50s and '60s, was certainly a nationalistic country. Perhaps historians will even call us a militaristic state. During this time when the potential for nuclear war was real, the decisions and status of the military basically were unquestioned. Most young men in my generation expected to serve in the military and did. Few in the airborne were drafted, and we all had the same level of commitment and desire to do our job. Ours was a generation in which service was not yet questioned.

One evening, while we were in a quiet period (no fighting), I could not sleep and was lying out in the open near my foxhole. In one of the unpopulated war zones, there were no lights, making the firmament more brilliant than I had ever seen it, even on the beach in Florida. I could examine the heavens in such great detail, and with time, my mind would drift across a great many subjects. Many of us were awake on those clear nights, searching for answers to our questions.

Our smallness, when compared to the universe, and the delicate position of our speck of dust made me wonder about how humans in prehistorical societies had thought about their place in the universe. Now facing an overpopulated world that seemed bent on exhausting its resources at breakneck speed, the willingness of man to face extinction by warring himself to death struck me as so fruitless. Looking at the stars through my military binoculars, I could not help but wonder about God: Is there one, and does he care? How could anything be responsible for so much? Religion is very much alive with men at war, but when war does not beckon, and the night air is clear, even the most unholy of men could not help but have thoughts and be in awe at what is around us. We simply need to see it and learn to understand who and what we are. We are mere children.

The men in the Kremlin (during this period of the Cold War), who could not see any other way, had the world poised on the brink of destruction. I had some idea, from my days in Germany, of how many nuclear weapons we had and a better idea of what they could do even if a few were used. It was also readily apparent that the Soviets had maybe as many such weapons as we did and would probably use them more readily. What a pity to shatter this world. If societies cannot coexist, why not just ignore one another? If we can't even do that, then perhaps we deserve an unappealing fate.

The proxy war we were in was difficult to swallow. Call it anything you like, but we knew it was not the real thing. Korea had already been forgotten, and the men who were sacrificed there were viewed with little more than idle curiosity. If we had to fight and die, many of us felt that it should be against the right enemy—the Soviets. Fighting an ill-conceived sideshow war in a forgotten and unimportant part of the world was depressing. We could not fathom the essential question of why we were there and what we were doing. On several occasions, my troops said they felt like paid mercenaries. In my view, the analogy was a good one.

This was not shirking duty in the least, but it was true that I really no longer knew why we were there and was not about to spout out some line of bullshit about dominos. Nothing would discredit me faster. The soldiers knew the real truth, and the futility of our mission was agonizingly apparent. To small unit leaders, motivation under such circumstances is perhaps the greatest challenge they can face. But on the other hand, we had a job to do, and we continued to do it well. Just not with the heart and spirit of our forefathers. Some officers did better than others at motivation, and some of the less enlightened did not know what was really going on, except fighting and the opportunity for their careers.

There also were other types of unsettling contradictions. We were winning the war, right? Well, yes, one would think so. We were certainly killing Vietnamese, uniformed troops from the North, and the guerrilla Vietcong from the South in record numbers and in far greater proportion than the casualties we were suffering. However, they had dedication and believed in their cause. They wanted to fight us; they came at us with stark fury. American troops who had operated with or knew the South Vietnamese realized that they would never be able to stand up against the communists alone, but most of us did not care in the slightest one way or the other. We just had to get through the day. The enemy had, in a way, seized the moral high ground. Our leaders had chosen the wrong war, made serious political missteps, and allowed the enemy to dictate the place and conditions upon which we would fight.

Our leaders assumed the struggle was military, whereas the communists knew it was more a political one with military overtones. In the U.S., the struggle had been reduced to McNamara's statistics. The simplicity of producing cars was the model since he had come from Ford Motor Company and, by the way, had been involved in production of the Edsel car. We were hopelessly outclassed (but did not know it then) by the men who were leading North Vietnam. Leaders in Hanoi had already won the intellectual aspect of the war; even world opinion was on their side. They were David, fighting the misguided American Goliath. This serious political mistake would cost those sent to fight, the sons of America, dearly.

The question of why societies go to war would return to me more than once. Still the concept of a nation sending its best young men out to die and underwriting such a venture with a misspent fortune cries out for moral justification, and we did not have that justification. The ills that would befall many a Vietnam veteran, even when we were there, had their germination in this problem.

We were soldiers, and we continued to function better than most American units. Not once did a soldier not do as ordered or what was right by our rules. We had not yet had to invoke a court-martial, and we guarded our record thus far as it was still important to us. Darker days lay ahead.

CHAPTER 7

MEDCAP

The U.S. Army had devised a system in which we would attend to the local medical needs of Vietnamese villages. The army called these medical civic action programs or MEDCAPs in military language. It was one of the U.S. Army's ways of winning the hearts and minds of the local people. By providing them with periodic medical care, some, probably those in Saigon or in the State Department, thought the Vietnamese population would see the light and be much more inclined to align themselves with the government/American side.

It was, as we said, a "nice try, but no such luck." We learned as time went by that even the Vietcong came to MEDCAPs, then sometimes ambushed the U.S. teams when they had completed their work and were on the way out. It was a naïve concept that this would work against so sophisticated an enemy as we were facing in Vietnam. It was very indicative of the arrogant and poorly thought-out manner in which we were approaching everything. Nevertheless, the take-charge American concept of fixing things in an empirical sense was in full swing. We were paying no attention to the minds of the Vietnamese, their society, or the character of their struggle, but we would drill their teeth or tend to their sores and hope for the best.

My company was assigned to provide a security detachment for a medical team that had been tasked to perform a MEDCAP in a small Vietnamese village. The two doctors and six medics involved in the MEDCAP were petrified to a man. We left early one morning in a convoy of some five lightly armed vehicles. Our MEDCAP was to be held in a small village about fifteen miles from the nearest U.S. or friendly position. The village was located in a heavily wooded area, and there were reports of light enemy activity around. A small MEDCAP would normally be a job for a senior sergeant or lieutenant. On this particular occasion, I took the security team and medical staff and assistants to the village, partly to observe an actual MEDCAP in action.

The local people seemed to genuinely appreciate the medical attention that we were offering and appeared to know that it was far and above anything they would likely experience again. A few even offered food, but they knew we would not take it. After about three hours, when most of the sores and skin conditions were treated, bad teeth had been extracted, and other minor ailments were taken care of, we passed out some propaganda leaflets and prepared to depart.

I had deployed a screen around the village, about five hundred yards out in all directions, and had good radio communications with each element. The two-man teams kept moving and checking with each other, all standard infantry tactics, but they detected nothing unusual. In fact, no problems of any kind were reported while the medical personnel were working. But a sixth sense was frequently your best friend, and mine was starting to send little alarms that something was not quite right. As we started to pack up and load the vehicles, the population suddenly disappeared. One of my sergeants noticed that the little kids were disappearing first; we knew trouble could not be far behind if the locals were getting out of the way. When the small kids disappeared, it was usually a good indication that something was wrong, and trouble was probably on the way. As near as we could tell, the Vietnamese had an admirable level of concern about children's safety, so much so that it was often a good alarm for us.

Even though we had not packed up everything and had left behind some field tables, medicine, and other gear, I felt that saddling up and getting the hell out of there was the smart thing to do. We piled into our vehicles and were on our way out of the village in a matter of moments.

Before we got back to the main road, I remembered noting a small dense patch of woods less than half a kilometer from the main road and thinking it would be an ideal spot for an ambush. As we got near the wooded area, it was clear that both my memory and my instincts were working in tandem. The area did offer excellent concealment for an ambush large or small. With what had already happened, I felt trouble was near; you could smell it. It was palpable in the air, and we were tight as bowstrings, anxious about what could happen. I stopped our little convoy short of what would probably be the killing ground. That somewhat unpredictable act apparently threw our unseen welcoming party off balance.

I had just stopped in the road, not quite in range, not quite in the area that was best for them to spring their well-planned ambush. After a few moments, it seemed to me that the ultimate precaution was to deploy the security team, which was an infantry squad of eight men. As soon as they moved toward the wooded area, firing broke out immediately. No one was hurt on our side, and we quickly returned fire with everything we had. I was using a 40 mm grenade launcher, which was very effective, along with a machine gun mounted on one of the vehicles and several M16s from everyone else. The squad was firing as well, and we appeared to be ready to take on our tormentors.

After our firing, we received no additional response from the woods. We were not an easy kill, so that had been a disappointment to the ambushers. They had disappeared back into the woods and the population. After a quick sweep, we found no enemy or blood trails. When we got back to our convoy and prepared to go on back to base, one of my men asked if this was the way the people of this country said thanks.

I had no answer for either of us. It was a complicated situation, not given to simple black-and-white answers or the impassioned solutions advertised by the champions of both sides back home. My vision was not so far reaching, but there in Vietnam, I knew some Vietnamese seemed to appreciate what we were trying to do, but it could well have been a clever mask. Others hated us, what we stood for, and what we were doing. Many other Vietnamese may have had family members soldiering with the Vietcong or as regular North Vietnamese troops. They had lots of troops, and they came from somewhere.

The dichotomies of war struck home. We did not know why Charlie would try to ambush us after doing a good deed like a MEDCAP. To us, it was a good deed and to the people we helped. But to Charlie and his leaders, it was simply a chance to produce more American casualties, perhaps cheaply. Clearly, the Vietnamese view of the war was different from ours. If they could kill a single American, it would swell the antiwar protest that much back home and give them more chance of staying the course and outlasting the U.S. It also could have been a simple action designed to illustrate to the villagers we had just treated who was really in charge. I did not know and could only offer my opinions. I did know that if we had not stopped short of the ambush site and taken the actions we did, we would probably have been killed.

In most ways that we could observe, it seemed to be a civil war that we were tangled up in. We did not live there, and we would not have to face the Vietcong at night alone in a village and explain what we did or did not do. I began to realize more than ever that we were fighting an entire society. We were fighting all of Vietnam, including the old, women, and children. It was like intervening in a family fight—you always lose. Our allies—the South Vietnamese, army, government, et al.—were corrupt and useless. The whole concept of what we were trying to do—kill the enemy—when the enemy was everyone, seemed terribly flawed and an unacceptable condition to me. It was becoming evident that this war was not winnable in the normal sense. Again, part of the confusion was that we were winning militarily by trouncing enemy units in the field. In the end, I thought it was clear that this would not count for enough. From my studies of war, even a young captain knew that there are many elements to war, and producing victory is a very complex undertaking. Destroying enemy units would not be enough.

Events like the near ambush of the MEDCAP were leading me to a place of mental certainty: that we should never ally with or fight for a government that was not worth fighting for. Cloaked in the all-encompassing anticommunist crusade, we—the United States—had made a terrible mistake. The government of South Vietnam was not a government; it was a collection of thugs. We operated with their soldiers enough to see what they were doing and how miserable their performance was against their opponents. We called the South Vietnamese "our kittens" and the North Vietnamese "their lions." Evidence of hatred toward the government of the South was becoming more obvious, especially when we were near any village or settled area. I knew then that the United States had made a dreadful mistake. We were backing an entity not worth fighting for. It was a corrupt government in all ways, but most importantly, it could not provide the motivation and causes needed and required to win a war. It could not and would not protect its citizens. The so-called government of South Vietnam was almost indifferent to the war. Even we lowly soldiers in the field knew this fatal weakness in our ally, the government we had been sent to save.

A new, more unpleasant phenomena encroached on my sanity after this little unrecorded incident, this misplaced, forlorn American effort to do the right thing. Perhaps despair, the emotionally chaotic and physically unstable world we lived in prompted the trembling and inner shaking to continue. No longer just a transient phase, it lingered for two days, complicated by particularly violent intestinal upheavals. My terrible dread was that this condition was becoming a permanent one. The anxiety caused by the waste, destruction, squandering of life, and the meaninglessness of our labors was the driving force of my maladies. In our gray, surreal world, nothing was clear, except our daily struggle to survive. Some of the men in my company thought it peculiar that "the cap'n was pukin' over there."

Some fellow officers asked if I was sick or what and then left it alone, much to my relief.

One simply could not pack up and go home as I sometimes fantasized about doing. No, we were stuck in our situation until we had done our time, and then we could board that big plane back to the world. It was not clear to me if the battalion commander knew of my particular vicissitudes or not. He did not mention it if he did and continued to act as though my company was the best in the unit. Certainly, no other officer knew, as one could internalize this kind of thing with a little effort. I knew a few of the men in my company knew, but they probably had much the same feelings and accepted it as normal.

As an officer, one takes a vow to uphold the constitution when sworn in and is commissioned by the Congress. I took that vow very seriously and as a personal pledge, not just an administrative requirement. I again promised to myself not to let my concerns about the war and my personal fears show. To do so would be to betray those trusted to my care. I had to do everything possible for them to preserve their lives, to get us all home.

We began to huddle together like condemned men. All we had was one another. We became protective of one another, brothers in battle, brothers in arms. Inadvertently, the U.S. Army had instituted a type of cohesion most American units did not have. The British and other European armies emphasized cohesion as the foundation of elite units. The U.S. Army did not, but it happened anyway.

In the jungle, you may have a small fight or even a major action, but the jungle would recover in days, not even taking serious notice of our efforts. While we could and often did lay great waste to the countryside, it had a marvelous way of saying "so what." It was another way, nature's way, of saying what we were doing amounted to very little. We occupied nothing, destroyed things that grew right back, and killed enemy troops and quite a few civilians along the way. In this scenario, we had to keep faith in one another and our abilities to survive our ordeal, or surely we would die.

CHAPTER 8

FEAR OF FEAR

America was engaged in a strange war and, by its very actions, was making it even stranger. There were no posters in the post offices, no slogans, no intense ideological force in our war. We were not encouraged to hate. There was no Remember the Maine or Pearl Harbor, no absolute evil such as the Nazis to declare against. Ours was a war, senseless, lacking emotion, drive, and the spirit other conflicts embodied. What we had as a national goal was characterized by pointless exertions, body counts, and dull repetition, and, worst of all, lies. Many felt that the war had cheated us of time and better experiences such as getting ahead in careers. Some soldiers nursed a sinister sense of grievance. It was clear even to the most unobservant soldier that we had been committed to a casual sideshow war. At home, there would be no rationing, no hardships or deprivations of any kind—guns and butter would be President Johnson's key to military victory. It left us singularly uninspired, unimpressed, and isolated even more in view of what we were experiencing.

This was bound to have a major impression on how one would react under the stress of combat. That is a question soldiers through the ages have pondered. I felt that my performance was acceptable, but some strange things—things I could not control—were starting to crop up. My teeth started to clatter (part of my overall tremors) in the aftermath of any kind of contact with the enemy; sometimes just seeing soldiers going on alert would produce similar effects since a firefight could easily ensue. This was a visceral level of fear and one that had to be masked and contained, and it would take great effort, increasingly greater effort.

It could have been that the type of war we were in was inducing this effect on my psyche, and the thought of dying a meaningless death was a powerful negative force. But as an officer, it would be impermissible to show fear, and I would be a failure if that crept through. It was there, though, in doses so large it felt like an anvil in the stomach. One could put up a good front and act as if nothing could faze me, but it was hardest of all to convince myself, especially with the growing certainty that we were all pawns in an awful national lie. The single hardest part was leading men in combat, giving orders, and sending men in harm's way. That was the most difficult thing, and I participated in as many of their duties as possible to alleviate my guilt.

One day while getting ready to depart on a patrol, my radioman, Steve, said, "Sir, we are risking so much for so little." That summed it up beautifully. We were taking the risks and dying. People want to cling to life, and soldiers are just young trained people, not automatons. Will today be the last one? As the sweat trickled off the tip of my nose while rechecking the map for the day, it splattered on the acetate covered map. I had been using a red marker and the sweat combined with this to present a nice red blob right where we were headed. Not a good omen. Soldiers are superstitious to a fault.

That feeling in the pit of your stomach, the sense that you were about to die, or find out if you were really a soldier or man. Either answer would be hard; nothing comes easy in combat. The suddenness of machine gun fire or a booby trap kept us always on mental alert, no matter what day or month or where. There was never a rest for the infantry in Vietnam—no rear area, no safe place. There were, of course, snipers, and they tried to seek out officers. There were minefields and booby traps, and there were simply single shots from the bush.

The intimacy of a guerrilla war grinds into the mind; it tugs at your sanity. You feel everything and everyone is there to kill you, and sometimes it is. It becomes a very personal, intimate war. We felt isolation and fear, and in the infantry, we felt separate from the rest of the military in Vietnam. Union troops at Cold Harbor marched shoulder to shoulder against withering Confederate fire, as had the Confederates at Cemetery Ridge at Gettysburg; and while that was just as deadly, it was far different from the day-to-day indifferent, anonymous encounters with death that we experienced.

When I was a child and after Uncle Steve had inadvertently given me directions, I felt I'd have to be a soldier and do what my country asked. Now it seemed that my country was asking a lot and sending all of us conflicting signals. The recognition that we were indeed fighting a hopeless war came slowly and painfully. It was hard for us to admit what we were feeling, that the war made no sense. Our cause had no soul or purpose. It is hard to motivate men to fight for a cause and all but impossible for a political abstraction and one we knew to be wrong. We could only try to survive. We were alien to the people who lived there, and we would simply have to kill them all to rid the area of communists. What was so appalling was the knowledge and certainty that the war was not only pointless, but that we were also on a fool's errand. I had been in Vietnam for almost seven months now, and reaching this conclusion was not going to make my remaining tenure any easier or more palatable.

This was not what America was all about; this was not what we should be doing. My soul yearned to scale Mt. Suribachi to fight real evil. I thought of our fathers who fought the Second World War and how their task was simpler. *They* knew; we did not. Their world was black and white; ours was all gray, a hazy deadly gray. Nothing seemed to fit; everything was off center. I could not believe this was the American way of fighting wars.

This was not the road to freedom, not the way to prove we had a better system than the communists.

Anguish began to erode my soul. Despair, like a cataract, was creating a film across my eyes.

The question of leadership is a difficult one at the lower levels. What is good, fair, and will inspire men is mixed. Countless variables range through the minds of small unit leaders. Few such situations are cut and dry. An issue arose—and it involved race—that was extremely difficult for me to deal with. As a Southerner, I made every effort to be fair (and probably overcompensated) in some of my decisions. Our battalion had been assigned a young black second lieutenant who was an artillery forward observer. His name was Cutler, and he seemed like a capable guy at first.

Cutler had been through the artillery school at Fort Sill, Oklahoma, but was not quite really ready for combat, not that anyone is. A forward observer is an artilleryman who lives and works with the infantry and calls in artillery fire when it is needed. He normally acts as an artillery advisor to the company commander, maintains his own radio communications, and has his own small forward observation party. This is a special skill and one that requires a good deal of coordination and common sense. He controls the major source of firepower for a unit when it is needed. The forward observer is a critical component for the infantry, as without him, you had no fire support; and in our situation, artillery could and often did make the critical difference.

When he became the forward observer in my company, I cautioned him about caring for his radio, having observed it lying on the ground in a puddle of water. As an officer, at least half of your job is being a teacher, and this normally requires patience, encouragement, and follow-through, plus a high energy level. In war, this is telescoped, and the luxury of time and patience disappear. A few days later, he took his three-man party into a crater while we were under mortar attack. I let him know in no uncertain terms that this was not a safe thing to do since a large hole with no overhead cover was dangerous if a mortar landed inside. The shrapnel would ricochet around and could kill everyone. He seemed to need more training. He was hesitant when calling in artillery and did not seem to know the correct procedures and methods of how to best employ our big guns quickly and effectively. But the battalion commander decided to send him to another company. Lieutenant Jackson was assigned to mine and became the forward observer.

Six weeks later, Cutler would be killed along with the two men of his forward observation party by a mortar shell in a crater exactly like the one I had cautioned him against taking cover in. His death left me in a terrible, sad quandary. I probably would have been more exacting on a white officer. Had this been the wrong thing to do? The question was not one that I would ever be able to answer; it became part of my baggage. Even though these men were no longer assigned to my unit, I still felt a sense of responsibility for them. Somehow, I felt I had not done enough; maybe more should have been done to train Cutler.

The limits on us were peculiar and reduced the options we would normally have. We were always on operations, so there was no time for training. But we had to be well trained to master the complexities of our war. It was a vicious cycle where poorly trained troops got killed or wounded only to be replaced by those with even less training. Finally, when soldiers got experience and were really good veterans, their twelve-month tour was up, and they went home. There is always learning in combat. The little and big things that can save your life and so on. But this always assumes that the basics are there, that replacements and even new units are trained up to a certain level before being sent in to combat.

While growing up, I had experienced prejudice, ostracized for being poor and having an alcoholic father. I did not like prejudice of any kind then or later. I was deeply affected by this childhood experience and promised myself I would never let such considerations affect how I looked at people.

In retrospect, I'd been too fair with Cutler. I should have had him pulled out of combat, had him given some additional training, and then returned to the unit, but I did not do that partly out of fear of being called prejudice. I wanted him to succeed and become good officer. War brings out the worst in all of us. Ultimately, we sacrificed this young man and thousands of others for the sake of expediency. We simply needed an FO, and no other considerations mattered at the time. It made no difference that he was black or white, experienced or not; he was simply cannon fodder like the rest of us.

CHAPTER 9

THE MYSTERY OF THE IRON TRIANGLE

Someone had referred to the Iron Triangle on the initial flight from Bien Hoa to Cu Chi on my first day in Vietnam. I had immediately pictured the cast-iron triangle that always hung from any homestead porch in the old Western movies. When an iron rod or a branding iron was swung through the triangle, it created a loud noise and was used as a bell for calling cowboys to lunch or for other alarms. Those adolescent memories were to be soon framed by a new definition: a triangle formed around a large portion of wooded no-man's-land fairly close to Saigon. There were several variations on what the iron part meant: Some said it was the iron (U.S. weapons) around the triangular area. Others claimed it was due to so much artillery blowing shrapnel into the ground, creating magnetic anomalies with our compasses, but most felt it was the triangular-shaped jungle area, much fought over.

As a quick-reaction battalion, we were sent in on an emergency air assault to rescue an American infantry battalion that was being cut to pieces in the Iron Triangle. As we neared the landing zone, a malodorous smell wafted up and swirled through the helicopter bay. In Vietnam, a bad smell was never a good sign, and the Iron Triangle smelled bad.

Diarrhea, the bane of the infantry, was a daily concern for me. Everyone else also seemed to have the malady. Perhaps it contributed to the overall smell. I was astounded at the filth we all lived in. No one got to shower since it was simply impossible under the conditions. We dry shaved in the morning, and we wore our uniforms until they rotted apart or simply wore out, which took only a few weeks because we slept, worked, fought, and did everything else in them. Most people don't think about where infantry sleep, which is usually on the ground, wet season, dry season, fighting or not. You sleep on the ground or in a shallow foxhole or, at best, a primitive bunker. Those men in rear-echelon units had most of the comforts of home, even though they may have been somewhat less than what would have been available in the U.S. This, coupled with the fact that the greatest danger they would face would probably be a paper cut, widened the gap between combat units and the rear weenies. More and more, we were becoming a young, draftee army. One that was being pushed to do its duty, not led by competent, crusading men in Washington or Saigon.

As part of the routine unpleasantness we experienced, the mere fact of having the runs could be fatal. After we got into the Iron Triangle and set up our positions on the first night, each company had established tight security; we had patrols out, listening posts established and reporting, and ambush locations around the battalion. In general, it appeared that we could handle most things the enemy might throw at us, short of a full-scale attack by several regiments. We had also laid in artillery (prearranged fire plans and artillery guns that already fired on selected sites to determine the exact range and improve the guns accuracy), and we had air strikes on call, had they been needed.

But it was dark soon, and the darkness of the jungle is special. It is blacker than black, and it echoes with strange sounds. It raises the sense of loneliness and envelops you in a new type of eerie embrace. You could not see your hand in front of your face. That is darkness, and it mirrored some of what we felt. In the heavy jungle, starlight and moonlight are screened from the ground by the trees. We were wrapped in almost pure blackness.

The company next to mine had a shy young trooper who did not dig a field latrine inside our position when he needed one, so he ventured outside our berm (the imaginary wall around us) in search of a private place to relieve himself and got disoriented. One of his friends said he could not heed the call of nature in front of others and would often look for an isolated area. He may have thought he was just outside his own position, but in the blackness of the jungle night, he walked in what appeared to be a semicircle—right into other positions of the battalion—the company next to his, and was killed instantly. There were more than twenty wounds in that young American from Oregon. He had died in a place with no name and for no real reason. Another family would grieve and feel the pain of a lost son. If mercy smiled and the darkness of the jungle prevailed, they would never know just how their son was lost.

Later that night, we were all nervous and on edge. It had started to rain again, increasing our discomfort and anxiety because the rain decreased visibility and sound detection even more. Our listening posts heard enemy movement, and we started firing mortars at the suspect locations. After what seemed like fifteen minutes or so, I got restless and went out in the now-drizzling rain to help the mortar crews unpack mortar rounds, cut fuses, attach the explosive charges to the mortar shells, and hand the rounds to the gunner. The mortar crews seemed to like to see an officer pitch in and do a little manual labor. The work was not too hard: opening the individual mortar shell canisters, getting the right amount of cheeselike propellant charges affixed to the tail fins of the mortar shell, setting the fuse, and then handing the shell to the mortar man.

It had only been ten minutes or so of work when the mortar crew farthest away from me took a direct hit from enemy countermortar fire. I got knocked flat by an American leg unattached to anything else but with the familiar boot and uniform. The mortar crew that took the hit was dead. Three men were killed, and several others nearby were wounded. I carefully tried to find the body the leg belonged to. I thought for a moment that I had it and realized that it was not a match. Mangled bodies, body pieces, screams, medics, the sickening smell of death, cordite, and jungle.

For the first time since arriving in Vietnam, I felt my control was slipping away, that it may not be possible to endure what was going on. Anger was building in my soul; a mean spirit and frustration were mounting. I started to walk back to my position and was near my foxhole when violent shaking overtook me, and my stomach came up with a fury I had never experienced before. Worse than seasickness or a bad meal, this was retching from the soul. In an unfamiliar way, my stomach and soul were to become like one, mere reflections of one another, connected and constant companions.

The callousness of people during war was amazing. One fellow officer, one of the other company commanders, laughed at me for getting sick after a firefight. He was the one who used a VC body as a map board for two days until the body decayed and the pins would no longer stick to the dead enemy soldier's back. This officer was a perfect example of fake machismo that I detested. Troops did not like it either. After I left Vietnam for good, I heard from another officer that this person had been accidentally wounded by one of his own soldiers. Such accidents can happen in the infantry.

As the monotonous days folded into weeks, my stomach never seemed to heed my brain. It was now an independent actor and out of my control. I had been in-country now for nine months. Prospects for the future were cloudy, except that we knew there would be more fighting. Most of the men really liked the boring days and took great relish in marking one more day off the list of days left in-country. It was a pleasant surprise to me that our morale remained high, and we retained our razor edge as a fighting unit. The next days were the same—orders, prearranged fire plans, air assaults, aerial observation, ambush patrols, booby traps, the sharp stakes of punji pits, incoming enemy mortar shells, air strikes, rice paddies, and the fatigue of war. Some days were like a training exercise, then others were just boring. We knew the boring days were a gift and that there would be many to come when we would wish to be bored.

The old World War II newsreels I had seen sometimes came to mind, and it was clear that they never reflected the hellishness of war, the war we knew. During this time, I had seen a South Vietnamese soldier who had fallen into a punji pit, languish, and die a death of horror without parallel. Punji pits were large deep holes, sometimes eight by eight feet wide and often six to eight feet deep, with sharpened bamboo stakes imbedded in the ground floor of the pit. The Vietcong would then smear the tips of the bamboo stakes with feces to make them in effect a biological weapon. The pit would be carefully camouflaged and waiting only for a victim. Sometimes the Vietcong would place a series of punji pits alongside a trail, then ambush a patrol coming down the trail, causing the victims to throw themselves on what they thought was the ground nearby but indeed was a punji pit. Thankfully, no movie could ever capture this kind of horror. All wars have horrors, but in a dirty war, one devoid of reason, such things assume a dimension all their own.

One of those difficult periods came after I had been in Vietnam for nearly nine months. For one reason or another, there was fighting almost every day. These were considered to be small engagements to the press or to the strategists in Washington or Saigon. But to the men involved in them, they were the largest battles in their world. Sharp clashes with deadly results: pain, anguish, agony, and death. I sometimes thought, *Are we the only American unit in this godforsaken place?*

I heard or read in the *Stars and Stripes* that in World War II, the average infantryman saw about 30 to 35 days of combat. Most of us were well over the 270-day mark now, and the end was not in sight. Many guys had a strip of paper, like a receipt from a grocery store, with numbers from 365 to 1 in reverse, so each morning they would cross off one more day and know how many more they had to go in Vietnam. One more day less to stay alive, one more day closer to home.

I wanted to go to a base camp and rest. My men needed uniforms. I could remember seeing pictures of exhausted soldiers in Korea and Germany during past wars. It was now clear as to why they had that exhausted look and what had given it to them.

After our combat operations in the Iron Triangle concluded, we headed back to Dau Tieng, our base camp. As we flew out on helicopters, I once again vomited (claiming airsickness) when sensing and thinking about what had happened while we had been there. We had not pushed the enemy back from Normandy, nor had we liberated anything. We had concluded another of several dozen repetitive and equally useless sweeps of the Iron Triangle. The enemy would return quickly, place new ambushes, set new traps, and bait us again. We could only claim to have destroyed the last few civilian structures in the Iron Triangle, nothing more.

On the flight out, I reflected a bit on what the Iron Triangle was and what it meant. It was a place of death. It was a place some of us would call a meat grinder because both sides fed additional soldiers in it to "wear the other down." So much for high-level strategy. One unit would find the VC, while another came in by air and would act as the hammer against the anvil. While effective to some degree, other tactics were simply attrition battles or search and destroy missions. These were simple World War I attrition tactics dressed up in helicopters and more modern weaponry in which we used up more Americans than we should have. With the tight control exercised over us from higher headquarters all the way back to Washington, there was no chance to develop one's own tactics and really take to war to the enemy. The airborne would have been particularly adept at this.

When we got back to the Dau Tieng area, we were again located near the giant Michelin rubber plantation. Rumors had been rife for months that the French were still at Michelin, or at least still in Saigon, and tending to their interests through surrogates. We also heard but had only sketchy evidence that the French, or at least their assistants, were helping the Vietcong when they could. The French were no longer for maintaining political control of Vietnam, but they appeared quite interested in their economic interests. To this end, they seemed willing to aid their former enemies and work against their NATO allies, a strange juxtaposition only De Gaulle could live with.

Up to this point during the war, we could not fire artillery or call in air strikes in the Michelin plantation without being in contact with the enemy, which is what we called a firefight. A firefight was contact with the enemy, and that could be large or small. It did not matter. Even if the firefight was a large one, we had to go through a rather difficult and lengthy approval process to use artillery or air strikes. Since only minor damage to a rubber tree was enough to kill it, we were instructed to be cautious, but we thought this was very odd. War is anything but environmentally sensitive, and we could care less about a few trees, especially if it meant our lives.

Rumor also had it that the U.S. had to pay some French company a handsome sum for each damaged tree. Basically, the full cost of the tree when it was producing sap. I could never prove it, and it may have been only a rumor, but I felt there were some who wanted good relations with the French, no matter the cost. This was an unbelievable turn of events—the U.S. was paying money in the form of damages to those who probably were helping our enemy, if the rumors were true.

It was during this operation that we got permission to fire freely into the Michelin plantation, finally adhering to the standard age-old rules of engagement: if we were under attack or saw enemy troops, you could engage them. Immediately after getting this welcome word, I heard firing coming in from several locations and on almost all sides and instructed the artillery forward observer to call in all available artillery fire. Others took note and did the same. Through most of the night, our one lone infantry battalion out in the middle of War Zone C felt like it was enjoying payback time, and we were venting our frustration. We fired enough artillery through the night to seriously damage about half the trees in the rubber, and we felt good about it. At least we could now defend ourselves to the best of our ability, and there was an unspoken satisfaction at being able to strike back at French interests that valued rubber trees over American soldiers. French interests who had, in the past, supported the cause of freedom, even in Vietnam and now with their heads in the sand, were assisting others in fighting the U.S.

CHAPTER 10

WHAT AN AIR STRIKE MEANS TO ME

Lying there as close to the ground as a body can get, smelling the dirt and almost becoming part of it, we heard the rattle of enemy guns. The American guns answered, deeper and longer, as we always had more ammunition. We were out near the Cambodian border on a routine sweep through the countryside, which was filled with beautiful, elegant teak trees that seemed to reach for the roof of the sky. It was a different part of Vietnam, no jungle, no rice paddies, but an open, lightly forested area. Poor soil and shade from the teak trees prevented dense undergrowth from forming, so we could see a long way, and movement was much easier than in other parts of Vietnam. It was such an attractive place, a mix of Northern California and part of East Texas.

It was late in the afternoon, in broad daylight, when all hell broke loose. The violence and totality of war overwhelms the senses, saturates the mind completely, voids out everything else. We were under attack; we were back in the war.

Enemy intelligence was good; they always seemed to know where we were and what we were doing. They knew we were not a fully equipped battalion but a mere morsel, easy pickings for them. This merely confirmed my impression that we were fighting an entire people. Everyone in the South was a spy, and everything we did or planned got right back to the senior officers of the Vietcong. This improved the tactical flexibility of those people immensely and gave them the advantage of selecting the time, place, and conditions for a fight. This helped them conserve their manpower somewhat and kept us on edge since we could never safely say there would not be fighting.

Those people in funny clothes—pajamas—were getting close, and they're coming at us, at ME. Their arrogance and foolishness were impressive. My next thoughts were of business—*goddamn ammunition, too heavy when you had it and never enough when you needed it. And where is the fucking air force?* One could not help but wonder if the enemy were smart or just arrogant.

We were on such a low-level routine operation that we had only three companies instead of our normal four. One company stayed behind at Dau Tieng on base-camp duty. Our heavy-weapons platoon was also back at base camp, training in the use of the 106 mm recoilless rifle and getting some additional machine guns. Our three companies were down to under 100 men each instead of the 144 authorized strength, so we were not as strong as we should have been and the missing heavy weapons folks made a huge difference in our firepower.

The first VC assault elements had been cut down as they moved forward. While they had inflicted some casualties on us, we were still in good shape, but it was starting to get dark. They came at us again, this time in small spread out assault packets (groups of four to six men, with assault rifles and grenades) trying to dissipate our firepower and get at us. These attacks came in from three sides and their idea was to weaken our perimeter, locate the weakest spot and try to penetrate there. If they could put enough of us out of action, their chances for success in this tactic would improve dramatically.

We were really in the soup this time, and when their assault strengthened, it began to make a difference. Our firepower started to drop off as we ran low on ammunition, and as our soldiers were knocked out of action. *We grew weaker, now near desperation, low on ammunition, out of artillery range, and there is no fucking air force around.*

The air force wanted to do strategic bombing from twenty thousand feet rather than low-level air strikes to support us. But bombing from high altitudes meant poor accuracy, which meant we would probably be hit from time to time, something we did not look on favorably at all. We liked the marine pilots best. They came from carriers out off the Vietnamese coast. You had to part the trees for those guys. They came in so low, but some of them had been infantrymen or at least served with combat units, and *they knew.*

With our wounded and dead numbers mounting, we closed our positions up as tightly as possible, and battalion headquarters became our reserve force. If the enemy broke through, the battalion commander and staff and the lightly wounded would be the force to throw them out. More than twenty men were dead according to a quick count, and another seventy to eighty were wounded, but maybe twenty of the wounded could still fight. Worst of all, three machine guns had been knocked out, and their firepower would be missed. Our defenses were now reduced by about a quarter by these casualties. Clearly, this was going to be a very long night.

Artillery fire would be useless if those people got inside our position since you would resort to calling fire on yourself only in the most desperate situations. This was an artillery technique I'd been told about, to call in artillery fire on your own position, theory being that if we were dug in and the enemy was not, he would suffer the most. It was a theory we were not anxious to try. Since we were out of artillery range (which rarely happened), it made no difference anyway.

If we did not get air support from the air force and get it soon, it appeared likely that we would be overrun. Once overrun, it would then be hand-to-hand combat. Next to death, the penultimate nightmare of the infantry is hand-to-hand combat. Our situation was grim, and each man was thinking of his own survival, his own little corner of the war, and the world. We knew the enemy had not used his entire force and probably was holding several companies or maybe an entire battalion in reserve. If they broke into our position and then used this additional force, we would not stand a chance.

I felt them getting ready. I knew the familiar sounds military units make when getting ready for combat—magazines being shoved home in rifles, ammunition loaded and adjusted, bayonets fixed, equipment tightened, and the hushed tones of orders being given. I could only think, *We won't make it this time. They are going to pour over us like a fucking tidal wave.* Thoughts of Arlington National Cemetery as a final resting place fleeted through my mind, and I thought about scratching out a will and leaving it in my helmet. I wondered, *Will my family miss me?* I'd promised them I would come home, and that promise seemed about to be broken.

The roar of jet engines screamed in above us. Two marvelous air force fighter/bombers rolled in at last. The aircraft looked like prehistoric silver birds of prey with their dihedral tail and drooping nose. Two, three . . . maybe four times. The large F-4 Phantom jets rolled in, ripping the larynx from the opera singer. One last time, for good measure, a pilot came in real low. We could smell the aircraft's exhaust soon after he went over and even read the writing on the fuselage of the airplane. Other air force jets arrived as the first duo expended their ordnance. The effect the air force had was total and devastating to our tormentors. The enemy had no ability to answer this awesome display of technology and timing. It was the perfect American answer to this problem. Technology, coordination, and careful execution, but lacking a central theme or purpose. It was tactics, not a coherent national strategy; and while we were winning the tactical engagements, the VC and Hanoi were beating us hands down in world opinion and the moral side of the war.

Hats off to the air force. They had done a superb job low and slow. I felt like saying, "You guys are as good as marine pilots," and our collective relief was beyond measure. But we hoped that the next time, it would not be so close a call. An air strike could mean life or death to that thin line of men in the jungle. It was our lifeline. The air force was our link with survival. Without them, we would have been overrun and probably all killed. Again and again, that night and at other times, I would think of the value of air strikes. They meant a lot to us. No combat pilot would ever have to buy a drink in our bar.

Why do men do the impossible under such conditions is beyond comprehension. I saw great feats of valor and sacrifice, and yet the cause was flawed. Everyone did their job; each did his best for his buddies and comrades, for the men he knew in his squad and platoon. Nothing geopolitical here, no grand strategy or dying for dominoes. Just loyalty to one another and to their best friends.

CHAPTER 11

BOOBY TRAPS AND HUNGRY MEN

After eleven months in Vietnam, we survivors had learned most of the tricks of the trade, those small but important things that helped us survive. Some were second nature, but all were important to know and use. We learned these survival techniques as quickly as possible, driven by necessity. We were playing a deadly game of chance. Men who frequently walked point (that first man out leading a combat formation, the tip of the spear) could even see a trip wire about the same thickness as piano wire even though it was camouflage colored and close to the ground; they could trace it and neutralize the explosive, artillery shell, bomb, or mine. An astonishing feat by any measure.

Others could hear mortars being fired from several kilometers in the distance and sound the alarm so we would all be able to get under cover before the first shells hit. Some had unbelievable instincts for predicting the locations of sniper positions, ambush sites, enemy positions, and the like. Everyone used anything they had learned to aid their buddies and the entire unit. We would spread the word about this craft and share experiences and knowledge with one another. Funny how it seemed completely normal to talk about booby traps, enemy bunkers, or firing positions and other devices of war in such a matter-of-fact manner.

I had hunted quite a lot in central Florida as a youngster and knew some of nature's warnings of human activity. When you were out on a deer stand, as a kid and by yourself, one's surroundings became intensified, and you learned a lot about nature. One day, our second day in the same location, we had already prepared our positions and been in them for over an hour. It was in the twilight of the day, and an orchestra of crickets were singing melodiously. All of a sudden, their special fiddling music stopped. I knew from my Florida experiences that men were probably on the move nearby, causing the crickets to stop singing. Thanks to hunting days in Florida, it was a clear and distinct warning that went off in my mind like a bell. Enemy troops are on their way.

I immediately alerted the first sergeant and the platoon leaders that Charlie was coming. Sure enough, in less than fifteen minutes, we had contact—bullets were flying. A brief little skirmish, probably no more than a dozen or so enemy troops. But there were no casualties on our side, partly because of the cricket warning. If we had been ambushed cold, we would probably have taken casualties. We shared our tips, hunches, and instincts as we went about our daily business of war and staying alive. This tip had paid off. Other tricks of the trade paid handsome dividends as well. One of the reasons we did not generally like replacements was that we knew they had to learn this craft, the life of the infantry, and learn it fast. Many did not.

After the firefight, my first sergeant came up to me and asked, "Captain, how did you know they were coming?" I told him that I learned about it in officer's training. He was skeptical and kept asking me for several days just how I knew Charlie was around. I did not tell him until a few months later when he was being evacuated on a helicopter with a nasty wound. Top had been shot in the stomach, but the wound was not fatal or even too bad. It was, however, a ticket home for him. As we got him on the helicopter, I said, "The crickets, Top, the crickets." He smiled a little now that he knew the truth, and he was in the air in moments, headed back to a field hospital and home. I had also shared this bit of knowledge with troopers who were in a position to use it.

Superstition was not uncommon either. More than one man carried a good-luck charm of some sort. Many carried small Bibles the military issued in their left breast pocket, thinking it may stop that deadly bullet. Others carried cards, mementos, charms, and even letters and pictures from home as good luck pieces. Some had strange good luck pieces, but no one ever questioned another man's choice of a life-saving lucky charm. Many turned to providence or God or anything else that would enhance their chances of survival. In addition to crossing off days as they passed by, some soldiers carried good luck charms, a picture of a girlfriend or wife or children.

Most of us knew that luck and chance were a key ingredients of survival, and these had been kind to those of us who had not been killed or wounded. But most of us would worry and experience disturbing thoughts over the perplexing and sometimes confusing reasons as to why we were being spared and our fellow soldiers killed. Our battalion had lost two officers by this time. One was a superb man, a gifted leader, smart, aggressive, and strong. The other was a person who should never have been an officer and died trying to be one. In combat, officers died just as readily as their men. Bullets, artillery, and the like did not discriminate at all.

It was at this time that we noticed when we returned to a position we had recently been in, the enemy would have been there apparently just after we left, looking for anything they could scavenge. We would sometimes double back in the hopes of coming up behind any enemy who was following us and maybe catching him off guard. In effect, the hunted was becoming the hunter.

Food was Charlie's big ticket item, but they would take and use almost anything. They would eat almost any food a

GI had thrown away, even the dreaded ham and lima beans. Charlie, we knew from experience, would make something out of anything useful we left behind. Sometimes they would hit the jackpot when a careless GI threw away or misplaced ammunition or something almost as valuable, such as an entrenching tool (small shovel). Since we were endowed with ample supplies, we tended to throw away a lot. Why carry something you did not need? Now a new tactic of circling back was designed to surprise the enemy at a time and place in which he would have lost some of his advantages.

With Charlie's scavenging in mind, we started punching holes in all the C ration cans we did not use so they would be spoiled and rot faster. The unit would dig one big garbage pit, not individual ones as before. Once the pit was full or just before we left, we would also dump in some tear-gas crystals to further discourage any junkyard dogs.

However, these were passive measures, and I thought it would be a clever idea to take a couple of empty C ration cans, pull the pin from a grenade (we had some grenades with only a one-second delay), carefully hold the grenade spoon down (the handle that flies off when the pin is removed and allows the hammer to strike the igniter/fuse and subsequently detonate the grenade), and slip it into the can. I tried one, and the fit was perfect. The grenade-filled can had to be inverted and carefully placed on the ground so that when someone picked up the can, the grenade would be freed, the spoon would fly off, and the grenade would detonate in a second—not enough time to get away. The can held the grenade spoon tight so it would not fly off while just sitting there. Overall, the fit was loose enough for anyone seeing a can, and reaching down to pick it up would get the can only, and the grenade would activate.

I got two fruit cans, which were the perfect size, and placed a couple of these booby-trapped cans carefully on the ground with a few other real C ration cans scattered about in a casual fashion so that it would look like the actions of typical GIs who didn't care what they threw away and probably similar to what Charlie had seen before.

It was another typical day in Vietnam, but this time, we had been warned of the possibility that enemy troops were close and indeed might be right behind us. When we departed our position, my company was last out the rear guard, and I was alert to any noise and had instructed all the platoon leaders to keep their men on guard as well. In less than fifteen minutes after we left the position, we heard two explosions in quick succession—they were the two booby-trapped cans I had left behind. *Gotcha, you bastards.*

All of us in the infantry suspected that the Vietcong tagged us to see where we were and keep track of our movements when they could. This was excellent and vital intelligence for the Vietcong. This incident was proof that they probably were always near us and frequently scoured our old positions. My company was sent back to screen our former position, so we took a different avenue back. We deployed in a diamond formation (an infantry combat formation), but when we went through our old campsite, it was empty. We found nothing but several blood trails.

The ability of the Vietnamese to move quickly continued to impress us all. We knew they had tunnels all over the place, but they still had amazing mobility even when we took this into consideration. In this instance, they were not familiar with the American tactics they were facing and did not like the booby traps that went off and may have been new to the area, so they beat feet out of there.

After all the booby traps, sniper fire, mines, and the other things visited upon us, our exacting a small amount of revenge on the enemy did not feel bad to me. In a strange way, it felt good to know that we were giving them a taste of their own medicine. For the next several days, I thought, *Maybe I got one of the bastards that killed one of my men.* But my relief was transient. We were not fighting for our national community or our families or our land, no greater good or ideal. We were just fighting. We were on a meandering course to a black void. We were achieving nothing.

We always watched out for booby traps and mines and any other clever devices the enemy could dream up. However, sometimes you can overtrain soldiers, and the ridiculous happens. We were on one of our short three-to four-day operations near Song Be in the foothills of the central highlands. One of the other companies was the lead company for the battalion that day. My company was to stay at our location and provide battalion headquarters security. We would rest, receive the resupply helicopters, and be the quick reaction force if anyone got in trouble. It was light duty, and we tried to keep it that way; and when the minimal work was done, the rest of the day was usually used for writing letters, cleaning weapons, taking field showers, and doing other housekeeping chores.

It was still early, and we were just starting the day's activities. Two companies had already departed the position, and the third was about to move out when we heard screaming and yelling in the distance. We could also hear equipment being moved or thrown about. Military equipment has a peculiar sound that one normally associates with combat. We naturally thought the unit was under attack and reacted accordingly. Artillery and aircraft were put on alert immediately, and we prepared to receive the companies back in the battalion perimeter. Troops under fire and coming back in to a position can be a tricky situation since you have to let them in and keep the enemy away. Everyone was tense and getting ready for a fight. Strangely, there was no firing after those first few moments, indicating something unusual.

Then just as we were primed and ready for combat across the open area where we had been the night before, the first infantrymen came bursting out of the woods. Each man had a large swarm of hornets in a frenzied swirl around him. Helmets were gone, and equipment and even weapons had been cast off in the soldiers' frantic attempts to get away from those aggressive, tormenting insects. As the men came pouring in to the position, we had some insect repellant spray, which we used liberally and got them into bunkers and under blankets as quickly as possible. Gradually, the stinging hornets disappeared, leaving most of us with a few welts. But those who had been nearest the hornet nest were in sad shape.

Our investigation discovered that a soldier from New York City had seen this large V-shaped thing hanging down from a tree. Thinking it was some kind of booby trap, this urban soldier quickly put a rope around it and, from a short distance, pulled down a giant hornet's nest. He had been near the rear of his company, and the second company was coming up, placing the hornet nest in the epicenter of the Americans. The results were incredible. Our battalion was declared combat ineffective for four days. It took almost an entire day for two companies, over two hundred men, to gather up all the equipment and weapons scattered through the woods while keeping alert more for hornets than enemy. We then went back to base camp at Dau Tieng, and people recovered from their stings. Several men had to be evacuated to Japan due to their reactions to the stings. One soldier was evacuated back to the U.S. and was said to have died from hundreds of stings, even some down inside his lungs. But we never received any official word regarding the truth of this account. After the hornet episode, we were very careful about such encounters and had even more respect for the jungles of Vietnam.

The soldier from New York who had inadvertently infuriated the hornets had his share of stings, but to compensate, he became a real student of various insects and snakes in Vietnam, and his family sent him information from various libraries. He became so good at it that we depended on his judgment. He said that after the war, he was going to go to college and get a degree in this topic. Amazing that even under such conditions, the human spirit will rise above it and find something good.

During fairly quiet periods like this, I sometimes wondered what it must be like for the North Vietnamese and Vietcong soldiers to fight the Americans with our incredibly deadly artillery and very dangerous aircraft. If there were combat with the Americans and if they survived the artillery and aircraft, they faced an infantry infinitely better equipped and supplied. Even if they were able to get through all of those obstacles, they would face an enemy who, on average, weighed between fifty to seventy-five pounds more than they did and was sometimes a foot taller. Vietnamese enemy troops should have felt like pygmies fighting Romans. Another of the strange realities of this war.

In a strange way, I also regretted having no substantial contact with the Vietnamese. In the war zones, where we were most of the time, anyone seen alive was a target. There were no civilians in the war zones. Even when we operated in areas with small villages, we frequently had no interpreter, and none of the Vietnamese spoke English. Most of them were terrified of the large, menacing Americans with their awesome helicopters, thundering artillery, and unusual ways. With these primitive farmers and under these conditions, there was just no opportunity for a dialogue. It would have been useful to have stayed near a village and been able to at least know something about the people we were supposed to be saving.

I remembered the MEDCAP and seeing the Vietnamese civilians who appeared like any other noncombatants. They had their own culture and ways of communicating and their own desires to live in peace and without invaders from thousands of miles across the ocean, from a place they had never heard of. They did not understand us, why we were there, and they were afraid to try to interact since it could be considered collaboration by the communists. Opportunities for normal human interaction were impossible under these conditions.

It was a sad commentary on the effect of war, but the Vietnamese, North or South, became somewhat less than human to me. With no understanding or meaningful contact, they were mostly obstacles we had to avoid and not hurt in a fight. But beyond that, they were faceless, mere parts of the landscape. U.S. troops, probably as the enemy, the invaders, were also seen in less than human terms to the Vietnamese. In fact, since we never really knew what side they were on, we sometimes referred to them as hostiles. To me, it was an entirely appropriate name. We were aliens in a faraway land, and this too had its effect on our feeling of isolation.

CHAPTER 12

A MOMENT IN A FIREBASE

After our rescue by the air force, we experienced no combat for over a week. Just patrols and moving to different locations, inspecting potential hideaways, looking for Charlie. Low-level activity, with essentially nothing to report, the boring side of war, but a welcomed one. We desperately need some downtime following our close call. Downtime to recuperate psychologically and even physically.

Then we walked in to a small enclave in the jungle hills, which clung like a festering sore to the side of a low undulating slope. Everyone was cautious as we neared the isolated American position. Such bases were usually well monitored by enemy troops, and they could ambush us on the way in or at least plant some mines or booby traps or even call in mortar fire.

The encampment itself was surrounded by barbed wire, mines, and barrels of fugass. Once we were inside, the air was fetid, and there were no showers. There was a lot of trash, and the place generally looked like a dump. We needed new uniforms, a hot meal, and maybe some beer before we headed back to the bush. Two or three miles away, there was a small firefight in progress, but we did not know who was involved and, sadly, were too tired to care this time.

The people in the firebase were a curious lot, somewhat like moles. Mostly they were artillerymen who had dug in and worried about surviving. The bunkers they made were supposed to be mortar and rocketproof, but they did not look that good. Men could get out quickly if they had to fire a mission to support the infantry and if their guns were not damaged.

On the other hand, most of us thought it was better to look for Charlie than the other way around. The people there had a desperate, sallow look. The only excitement of their days was the infrequent requests for artillery fire from beleaguered infantry units. I preferred the bush to this type of life. The firebase folks viewed us as insane gladiators, and when we prepared to embark, we got a few well wishes, stares, and some jeers since soldiers always have a way of taunting one another. Even though we were all combat troops, our roles were quite different. In all likelihood, most of those men, had they been given an opportunity, would have gone with us rather than remain in squalor, passive targets awaiting an enemy who might never come. If Charlie did come, it would be with overwhelming force, and the firebase would probably be overrun in minutes, or perhaps it would take longer, but Charlie would not attack unless sure of victory. These people were vulnerable, and they knew it.

In our brief stay at the firebase, a young man from Michigan deliberately blew part of his hand off. I spoke with him briefly. He vainly tried to apologize, agonize, or rationalize his actions. From my perspective, self-mutilation was something for other armies, those without a soul. It was sad to see such an event in the American Army. I felt a deep humiliation both for him and the country. Another man with a ruined life would return home. He would never forget or forgive himself; he would be a casualty just as sure as if the Vietcong had blown off his arm. I thought of those who refused to serve in the military and instead went to Canada; they too would be casualties but of a different kind.

He had tried, this young man, but could do no more. None of us felt anything but pity. All of us knew we could be overcome in the same way. *What a waste.*

Once again, my old stomach malady friend visited me, but I had made it to a latrine before throwing up, so the embarrassment was lessened. It was not combat, not even the sight of more blood. It was the thought of another wasted man, another wasted life for this war. Again, it was the lie we were living, the mindless war we were executing that made one retch.

Early the next day, we received new uniforms and boots and, of course, C rations via helicopter resupply, exchanged some weapons, loaded up on ammunition and soft drinks, and were ready to saddle up. The battalion commander said we would depart early the next morning. The operations officer had an idea that we would be operating in War Zone D, the worst of the war zones, because it protruded like a finger into the Ho Chi Minh trail, our enemies' vital supply line. Heavily wooded and with only a few logging trails, it was considered a difficult place for us to fight in. Any American activity in War Zone D almost always got quick and determined enemy attention, and heavy fighting was the normal result. But we would go where we were ordered to go, even with a heavy sense of foreboding.

Suddenly, with no hint or warning, several mortar rounds ripped into the firebase, one scoring a direct hit on a 105 mm howitzer. No ammunition was detonated, and it looked like the gun could be repaired fairly easily. *Fuck Charlie, he is not serious this time.* A few moments later and just as suddenly came the heavy machine gun fire. *Now that was serious.*

The battalion reacted, assembled into combat formation, and prepared to head out. My company was second out the gate and back to the bush. It had been a strange and brief interlude interrupted by business as usual.

As soon as we departed, the enemy firing stopped. We searched for the source of the mortar and machine gun fire but found little to follow up. Elusive as ever, Charlie had been tailing our battalion; and when we came to rest in the firebase, the collective target was just too tempting for him to resist. Charlie was now also holding his fire until we got a resupply or medevac helicopter in our position, with the idea that he might get a lucky shot, bring down a helicopter, and cause even more casualties.

We began to notice that he seemed to have more ammunition of better quality, and when we captured some ammunition, it was straight from Russian factories and only a few months old. More rocket-propelled grenades (RPGs), the famous Soviet designed antitank weapon, were showing up, and the heavy mortars, up to 120 mm, were also becoming more common.

The RPG was an interesting weapon. An outgrowth of the German Panzerfaust of World War II, it consisted of a launch tube with a simple sight and firing mechanism. The round consisted of a rocket motor, which gave about a two-second burn, long enough to propel the missile to its target. The business end was a shaped-charge warhead on the front, which was designed to destroy a tank. A soldier could carry one with several rounds and become a poor man's artillery for his compatriots. The RPG packed a serious punch—it could tear through armor, completely destroy an armored personnel carrier, or utterly waste a bunker of any type. Ideal for close-in fighting, the RPG was cheap, light, rugged, simple in design, and deadly in effect. It was in many ways a perfect weapon for the Vietcong, and they used it well.

All of this told us that the air force, despite a very valiant effort, was not winning the interdiction battle. Plenty of supplies were getting through, and we were literally feeling it. It also told us that the special forces actions, in conjunction with native tribes in Laos and central Vietnam, were not accomplishing what they were designed to do. Their mission had been to fight the North Vietnamese coming down the trail and to make allies of other tribal elements and turn them against the North. It was already apparent to any knowledgeable observer that we were fighting most of the people in the country, North and South.

Now evidence was stark and plain—we had proof that supplies were readily moving from North to South. Ammunition that was only a few weeks or months old obviously had not been stored for long or built up in supply dumps over a period of time. Clearly, it was coming down a wide open highway. This could only be done if Southerners were willing accomplices and indeed probably even acting as porters. Movement of supplies and men down the Ho Chi Mihn Trail was a complex and difficult undertaking, and it was being done by a vast network of people in North and South Vietnam.

I thought again that it was too bad we did not have some congressional lawmakers here to witness what we were seeing, to be confronted by some of these facts. Had they or their staffs done some serious, penetrating investigative work of that type, the political direction of the war would possibly have taken a dramatic turn. Why is it that no one, not even many in the press, would venture out to the lonely units on the cutting edge? We never saw any senate staffers or staffers from the house, even though plenty came to Vietnam. The questions were patently obvious and so were the answers. But I think most of them stayed in Saigon, where it was safe. They were well briefed and had a good hotel with all kinds of amenities. So much for finding facts and inducing a good deal of cynicism.

America's leadership could have availed itself of some honest, unscripted answers that the men in the infantry could have provided. It should surely be a crime to send the nation's youth to fight a war in a distant land and then not even have the concern and dedication to understand what they were doing and what was actually happening at the lower levels. It is frequently said in history that the man rises to the hour, but for the U.S., the hour had come, but no man had been found to give us the ability to win the war or get out of it. We had not a Churchill or Lincoln.

This was symptomatic of the entire American involvement in the war. Some good information was undoubtedly getting back to decision makers in Washington, but it was not enough. Without a true picture, they could not form a coherent strategy, and without a coherent strategy, we were compelled to fight for only tactical advantage, not win the war. The dog was chasing his own tail.

The war protests were growing daily, and it was clear that they had their own message. We saw the signs saying, "Hell no, we won't go," the demonstrations that were getting more massive and including more people from all walks of life. The campus riots were particularly disturbing since these were people our age. The draft was coming closer to many of them, and they simply would not serve in such a complex war, which many saw as useless and needless. Nevertheless, most of us in combat harbored no ill will toward those carrying signs instead of rifles. I asked many men what they thought about the hippies who were taking to the streets. Many had no opinion or at least not one they would share with an officer. Others, however, said that if they were home, they may well be in protests against such a crazy war. Others said they were traitors, but probably were just misled. No one seemed to want to throw them in jail or see them harmed.

One soldier from New York offered a bit of compelling logic. He said we were both fighting, just using different tools, and that the real problem was that those in charge didn't have a clue. I talked to this soldier into the night and found that he was far more politically aware than most officers. Once again, I had it driven home to me that you simply cannot fool an

American soldier, no matter how sophisticated you think you are or how clever your staff may be—the guy on the ground will know the truth. Our fathers did not **want** to fight World War II, but they knew the truth and acted accordingly. They knew their cause was both right, and for freedom, we only knew we were fighting.

The corrosive, demoralizing effect of knowing you are fighting for nothing is hard to overestimate. My mind raced ahead, searching for a remedy to protect our country from senseless wars in the future. I thought of one of my college professors who lectured on constitutional law. Fervently and naïvely, I thought we should amend our constitution to have a law prohibiting any president from sending troops to war, unless he himself has served in one—and I mean served in a real capacity, in the infantry. Then I went back to the business of fighting again.

CHAPTER 13

A FLEETING MOMENT, A DEATH

He was a young boy made soldier by his country, and like most, he came from a loving, caring family back home. His father had somehow managed to send him a .357 Magnum pistol to be used for close-in protection (M16s were too bulky and cumbersome to use for very close-in combat). Perhaps the father had been in the Second World War and knew the use of a pistol. In all likelihood, it was a desperate gift of love and concern for a son far away, in the forlorn hope that somehow it would help preserve their family's stake in a cruel war. They would learn, as would thousands of other families, just how cruel and bitter the war in Vietnam was to be.

Lots of guys wanted to have pistols because Charlie always tried to get close to or even into our positions. For them, getting in close took away much of our ability to get effective air strikes and artillery on them, and they were our most potent weapons. When we were under attack and if Charlie got too close or was inside our positions, a pistol was an ideal weapon. In the dark, a pistol could mean the difference between life and death; and in the confusion of night fighting, it could be of great use. A secret of the trade that only an infantryman would know, and his father must have known. The army issued pistols only to officers and the battalion sergeant major as sidearms. Each person in a military unit got a basic weapon, and the M16 was issued to most.

Most people don't realize that you rarely see the enemy, and most combat is by sight or sound, firing back at muzzle flashes or sounds. In our war in the jungle, combat was closer and frequently at night, but even there, we did not often see Charlie, except when we found bodies. In more open areas, combat could be at ranges of hundreds of yards or more. But at night and in the jungle, Charlie would try hard to get within fifty feet or less of our positions. That would be close enough to rule out effective air or artillery strikes. Then if he outnumbered us, he would stand a good chance of destroying us.

Combat soldiers are usually young, averaging about eighteen. Immaturity would sometimes show up even in a combat zone, and one sign of this was a tendency for one to show off guns or just play with them.

I detested pistols and grenades and most of the tools of our trade. Used without the utmost care, they would be entirely indifferent as to whom they killed. I saw what they did; I knew what they were for and when we would use them. Close-in combat was the worst of all the things we endured. But in that scenario, they were useful tools.

The young soldier did just what young men sometimes do; he had been playing with his pistol, then carelessly put it down on a C ration carton. He never thought his friend would pick up his pistol, assume it was not loaded, cock the hammer, point it at him, and pull the trigger. Just like a couple of ten-year-old boys playing cowboys and Indians. The friend thought it was a joke until the pistol fired the loud report, the recoil.

The bullet went in the young man's upper right chest and ripped a gaping hole through vital parts and came out his back. He lived for a few minutes and died screaming in agony on the side of an unnamed hill in the middle of a jungle no one cared about, in a place where we should not have been.

Another bright young American was dead, painfully, wastefully, and stupidly. This was the second time I hoped fervently that parents would never have to deal with the truth of how their son had been killed. It was bad enough for us to know, but how could a mother ever accept such a thing?

In reality, two bright young Americans were dead. One was in a body bag; the other would carry the scar of his mistake until the day he died. He would never escape no matter what he would do, no matter what he would try, achieve, think, or become. He would remember that moment of death for the rest of his life. He was another destroyed person. No visible wounds, no body bag, no statistic, but a casualty nevertheless.

I walked over to see the body before the helicopter came in to pick him up, just another body bag. My mind was reeling with a numbness, as when you wake suddenly before you are rested and have that momentary disorientation of not knowing where you are. It was difficult to accept that another soldier had died. Even more so when the death was pointless, without a shred of meaning or purpose.

True, infantrymen live with weapons; they are our stock and trade. One can't help but ask how could something so stupid happen? Older, more mature soldiers even asked me exactly that: How could this happen? To me there was another level of guilt and responsibility here. Our government, our president, had sent us here, and this was one of the prices we were paying. This was no longer cowboys and Indians. This was real, and men were dying.

In the search for the true definition of war and its meaning, purpose, and why humanity does it, some thoughts came to mind. War is the animal man at his worst best; the thin veneer of civilization is gone, stripped away. We were reverting back to savages in thought and deed. Hollow warriors standing on a monument to a level of culpable insanity I never knew existed.

CHAPTER 14

WITH ALLIES LIKE THESE

After the long months in Vietnam, I felt somewhat seasoned, but there were often events you simply were never prepared for and I don't think you ever could prepare for. We had moved to a heavily wooded area—known as the little red schoolhouse—between War Zone C and War Zone D. The little red building was not really a schoolhouse but probably an old tollhouse or customs building on one of the roads going from Bo Duc, Vietnam, to Cambodia. It got tagged as a schoolhouse, and the label stuck. Our area of operations was not exactly a friendly place, but there were no signs of enemy activity and no intelligence indicating the presence of VC or North Vietnamese, so we were not expecting any immediate fighting.

We were fairly near the district capital of Song Be, in a part of Vietnam where the dirt is full of iron ore, giving it a distinct bright-red/orange hue. When a helicopter came in to land, it would kick up billowing clouds of fine rouge dust. Only rain would calm the dust for a period of time or relieve us of our newly acquired color. It was a distinct change from the green of the rice paddies and jungles we were so used to. An amazing country with more than average variety and even more contradictions.

Once we had selected our position for the evening, we began to dig in and prepare for any action that may come that night. About an hour before dusk, the first few mortar rounds crashed into our position, and we assumed we were coming under attack from Charlie. Shells kept coming in at the slow rate of only one or two every few minutes. But there was something odd. We could hear the shells coming in, but there were no explosions. Even though the shelling was slow, too many shells were coming in. Charlie rarely had such ample ammunition supplies, and when he did, they were for something big.

Finally, one shell hit and bounced into the air rather than going several feet into the ground, allowing us to get a quick look at it. The shell was a U.S.-made canister, one that held propaganda leaflets rather than high explosives. A few of the leaflets had come down in our position, and a quick study of them indicated that they were from the South Vietnamese Army.

Frantically, we began to call everyone we could on the radio to get the shelling stopped. Shells continued to rain in near our positions. Our luck ran out when a soldier was hit in the upper arm/shoulder by one of the artillery shells, and it ripped his arm and a portion of his shoulder off. One quick look told me that there was no chance for any type of medical reconstruction there. In fact, he was quite lucky to be alive—a few millimeters more and the wound would have been fatal. An empty 105-millimeter howitzer shell casing weighs approximately twenty pounds and can easily be a deadly, deadly bullet when propelled through the air.

All we could do was lie low and hope the shelling would stop, but perceptibly, and to a man, our mood began to change to anger. Our sense of urgency did not seem to be reflected by those we contacted on the radio. No one, including our higher headquarters, seemed to know who was doing the firing. Others we contacted, such as district liaison did not seem to know either. Then we started receiving volley fire—six rounds at a time. In desperation, I got out from cover and plotted the back azimuth of the artillery shells so at least we could try to locate where the firing was coming from and have our mortars or artillery support unit shoot back. I located what seemed to be a good artillery position on the map and at about what I thought was the correct distance and called in a fire mission.

Our artillery began firing a single round of white phosphorus each minute and timed it to detonate at two hundred meters over the position I had called in. After a few rounds from our artillery unit, the empty shell casing ceased cascading into our positions. I remember thinking at the time how artillery shells really make only a minor amount of noise, unlike some long, slow freight train in the air that I had thought would be their signal.

Later we found out that a careless and poorly trained South Vietnamese artillery unit firing propaganda leaflets had failed to calculate where the empty shell casings would fall. They fell on us. This lack of coordination really bothered me. I knew we (Americans) tried our best, even took casualties to avoid hitting Vietnamese civilians and were very careful not put fire on South Vietnamese units.

My battalion commander was more than irritated at me for firing artillery at them and was of the opinion that we should have waited and let the Vietnamese unit be contacted. I also had threatened to take personal action against whoever was firing if it did not stop. Another officer who overheard me call in a fire mission on the unit firing on us and was safely located in a major American installation (Tay Ninh) told me I was being unprofessional.

Many in the U.S. Army in Vietnam liked to emulate the cool fighter-pilot attitude depicted by Chuck Yeager. Usually, this demeanor applied when they were well out of any kind of danger. This type of phony behavior irked me more than most since I always felt it was easy to be cool and calm when you weren't in harm's way. When someone is trying to kill you, whether they mean to or not, it gets your blood up. You do scream and yell. *Screw professionalism.*

It seemed like killing the infantry was becoming a sport. We were starting to feel like hunted animals. The huge, bloated American staffs and headquarters back in Saigon, Bien Hoa, and at dozens of other places in Vietnam had little real idea of what we were experiencing. When draftees could ask an officer why "all those guys back there can't figure out how to run the war better," it was a clear indication that they were not doing the job at hand. Many officers and others avoided field service, and few seemed concerned about the lot of the tired and dirty infantry. We were expendable, and it was starting to show too much.

Once again, my involuntary reactions began, shaking and trembling all over, no longer just my hands. My entire body was quivering. My teeth clattered, and I hoped no one heard. My bones were shaking deep into the core of my soul. Nausea swept over me like a hurricane; there was an odd sensation at the top of my stomach. I thought of the then-popular Glen Campbell song, "Galveston," where he sings, "I am so afraid of dying." I never knew what real fear was before. I was very, very afraid. *If I am to die, it should be for a cause, for home and hearth, or something worthwhile, but not this.* Our fears were compounded by uncertainty and clouded by incidents such as we had just experienced. Such events were troubling enough had they occurred rarely, but it was becoming all too apparent that they were not that rare and not always excusable.

CHAPTER 15

TO KILL THE THOUGHTLESS

We had left War Zone C and moved south into a position along a wood line in the area west of Saigon and just north of the sprawling Mekong Delta, near a small hamlet called Go Dau Ha. In front of us was an open area of rice paddies about a mile across, with a meandering, fetid stream in the middle. There were rice paddies on each side of the stream, and off in the distance across the paddies and stream, there was a heavily wooded area. We would be moving into the wooded area the next day and sweeping it for signs of the enemy.

The wooded area bothered me. Without proper reconnaissance, it would be an excellent place to ambush us, and we could stumble into it without warning. It would have been my selection for cover had the situation been reversed.

My opinion to the battalion commander that we were asking for trouble by crossing that area—it was a great ambush site—a perfect instance of the valley of the shadow of death. If we could not conduct a reconnaissance of any type, then I suggested that we blast the hell out of the woods with some concentrated artillery fire and call in air strikes just to make sure we were not getting into trouble.

The battalion commander and I went back to the district headquarters (Vietnam had districts that equated roughly to counties in the U.S.). At this headquarters, an American captain told us we could not have permission to fire artillery into the woods on the other side since there were no enemy in his district and he was concerned about collateral damage to the economy in his district. Heavy fighting could ruin crops, buildings, and cause civilians to flee an area. His province was prosperous, and he wanted to keep his record successful. After about an hour of wrangling, he refused our request and said we were worried about nothing since there had been no intelligence about VC in the province. This was not the first time we had heard there was no intelligence about something.

Dislike of a person can take many forms, so I got right in his face and asked him to join our battalion. Since we would jump off or begin our movement early the next morning, he could observe our maneuver, and it would be all the better since it was in his district, and we would be perfectly safe, and he would be back in his nice building in time for lunch served by pretty Vietnamese girls. He declined, saying he was too busy.

Once more, before leaving, we asked about the possibility of Charlie being in the area. We got the same reassurance. This captain and others around him then departed to their comfortable bunks and prepared meals. Their luxurious, smug life was alien to us, and their self-assuredness was not convincing to us infantrymen. They were garrison troops. I knew I was strung out, that my judgment was becoming impaired, but it was irrelevant. Before we left, I went over to the captain. Since we were the same rank, I told him that if my unit came under fire and took casualties and if I lived, there would be a score to settle with him personally.

We flew back to our position by helicopter and settled in for the rest of the day. The next morning, at about 8:00 am, we moved out as planned. We made it about halfway across the open area just short of the stream, and the enemy in the woods that looked like a good ambush position opened up with all he had. We were now pinned down by an incredible volume of fire. My company and half of another, some 200-225 men, were stuck, and the rest of the battalion could not move. We were simply sitting ducks. After several mortar rounds were fired at us and what seemed like thousands of rounds of rifle and machine gun fire, there was a sudden calm. I waited for the infantry assault that Charlie should mount. My unit was spread out, having trouble communicating, and we were lying in warm water of rice paddies exposed to the sun with little cover. Firing began again as we tried to suppress their weapons, but no infantry assault came. They had us pinned down and were making the most of it. As we lay in the water, the heat of the day was just beginning to ratchet up.

Heat in the jungles and lush green rice paddies of Vietnam and South Asia is not like the heat of summer along the humid East Coast of the U.S. The heat here penetrates all the way into your mind; it affects how you think, drags on you like a wet blanket. It cooks the head inside your helmet, makes things you touch searingly hot, and keeps you lathered in sweat most of the time. We smelled bad, we looked bad, and most of us felt bad, a peculiar situation for young men at the top of their physical prowess.

The prevalence of water and the frequent rains register a humidity level that is near 100 percent for several months of the year, the rest of the time it drops imperceptibly lower. The heat adds to our misery, and along with the insects, leeches, snakes, scorpions, and bats, it seemed like Vietnam was truly a hellhole. Certainly, it was not a place any of us would consider worth dying for.

I lay there in the filthy water, cursing the son-of-a bitch captain who would not give permission to fire preparatory artillery in his district. We began to test enemy fire by lifting helmets on rifles, and we quickly found out that Charlie was very much still there. Thirst began to work its way into my senses. I pulled out a canteen and discovered it had a bullet hole right through it. By midmorning I drank rice paddy water. Rice paddies are septic fields in Asia, but in war everything exchanges the absolute for the relative. I was thirsty, and the fact that I could get sick from the water was irrelevant to me at the time. Fortunately, I did not get sick, probably because the rice paddies we were in had been dormant for years and nature had cleansed them enough for consumption.

Finally, just after noon, the air force arrived, silver birds with green bombs of death. They struck the enemy positions, and they struck hard. With napalm still burning, we assaulted what was left. We came up out of the paddies like men possessed, John Wayne if you would. We were not going to die there, not like that, pinned down and helpless. We simply went forward without specific orders. We all knew what to do, and we were all comrades looking out for one another. Our teamwork was paying off; we believed in one another.

Camaraderie was a vital component for us during this critical situation we had been put in; it was about the only thing that could enhance our fighting efficiency.

Vietnam, for the soldiers who fought, broke down any economic or social barriers. None of us took any notice or care about who was black or white, who was rich or poor, who was educated or not. We were all simply army green. This interdependence, coupled with our own tactical initiative and expertise, something the army stressed, gave us this kind of enormous fighting capability. We acted as one out of concern for all. Again, we were actually better than the Vietnamese military, and we were winning the tactical war, but only the tactical war.

After we secured the woods, searched, counted, and buried the enemy bodies and prepared our positions for the night, I got on the next helicopter flight back to district headquarters. I was in the worst frame of mind I had experienced since arriving in Vietnam. Two good, brave men had been killed and three wounded for some arrogant, stupid officer's vanity, poor judgment, and cowardice, and I wanted to get the little bastard who was responsible for this travesty. I had become a grim, dangerous infantryman and a person who knew all too well how to kill. The battalion sergeant major said he needed to go back to district headquarters to file our combat report and was with me on the flight. He later told me he knew exactly what my intentions were and why I was going back as he had heard about my confrontation with the captain. When we landed, I walked over to the captain's tent, took out my pistol, chambered a round, and started to go inside. The sergeant major who was a step or two behind me knocked me flat, and a couple of others took my gun. An idiot lieutenant colonel appeared and threatened to court-martial me. I barely paid any attention to him. His uniform was spotless and ironed; his boots polished. He was a garrison soldier. He did not have that look in his eyes, the look of the hunter or the hunted.

I had failed to find the captain who, upon hearing I was coming for a visit, had gone into hiding; I could only go back to our position. I told the colonel to come out to the field and press court-martial charges if he liked. A comment I felt safe in making since rear-echelon types did not like to come out to the field since it could be dangerous out there, and they might get dirty. I also said that "if I ever saw the 'courageous' captain again, I'd still settle the score then and there, make right what he had fucked up, let him experience firsthand what our day had been like, what he had caused."

In retrospect, I knew deep down inside that I really wanted to kill him and probably would have, given a chance. War is waste; it corrupts the mind, distorts one's values. "The absolute for the relative." The pain of the moment is incredible, magnified. You cannot control events around you, and it begins to move you toward what would otherwise be illogical acts. Our lonely duty was eating at us all.

It also crossed my mind that I owed the sergeant major a great deal for what he did. I could easily have put myself in prison, but he had the good sense to prevent that. He had taken a risk, struck an officer, and there were witnesses. He had kept his balance better than I had. Sergeants are frequently called the backbone of the army, and in this case, it was certainly accurate. Later, when I thanked him, I told him that if he ever needed anything from me, it was his. He was a good man and a very good NCO, and we needed men like him.

On the flight back, I noticed, to my dismay, that I could no longer hold a pencil well enough to mark out our positions on battle maps or even to write notes. I resorted to jotting or scribbling down half notes or key words, hoping that I could reconstruct the entire text later. I remembered thinking, *I'm just about at the end of my tether*. Little did I know then that my tether would not end here, but it would be stretched further and further. I started thinking about the book *Catch-22* and could not help smiling at the thought of Yossarian being here in our world. It would be nice to get to know him under these conditions.

Complicating this was the political situation in the U.S., which was increasingly bothersome to a lot of the men. It bothered me too. If the U.S. was having so much trouble and so many people were against the war, with more joining the protests daily, how could we expect to carry this thing through? There was no home front like in World War II, but to have an "anti" military back home was very disturbing to us. We all knew that we were bleeding in vain, sacrificing for an abstraction of questionable value.

While my battalion and I think most other combat units were fighting well as teams, and in fact we were beating the Vietcong and North Vietnamese soundly, there was no coherent strategy above us other than the tactics of the day. The allied structure was a joke, and we were being beaten badly in the propaganda field. I also thought that what we had been told to do reflected a major disconnect between the military and our civilian government leaders. Something was not working, and it was becoming more apparent daily.

It was a good time to reflect on what the men in the company thought of their leader. There were several men I could ask, and I knew I would get a straight answer. The first sergeant and three others told me the men in general respected my anguish over their situation and the fact that I tried to look out for them. Some few felt like I may have gone off the deep end or maybe was just tired. We were all pissed, so that did not matter. But they still had faith in me, and that was all I needed to know.

Elliott with AK-47 from 15 year old NVA he killed at Soui Cut

Elliott, showing the despair of impending defeat

Fuel dump at Cu Chi, destroyed by VC

Machine gunner at work

Officers call, War Zone C, Elliott on far right

Typical enemy bunker

CHAPTER 16

OF ROME PLOWS AND AGENT ORANGE

We experienced a few weeks of relative calm, and there was some time to reflect and observe on the events of the past months. Some of the more amazing sights we had witnessed were the American engineering projects under way in Vietnam. The United States was at war and applying its massive engineering skills to the topography of Southeast Asia. We were literally changing the landscape in numerous ways.

To reduce the chances of American units getting ambushed, the engineers used what they called Rome plows—giant tractors that plowed and ripped up large swaths of jungle alongside the roads of Vietnam. The scar on the land was incredible; it went for miles and made power line easements in the U.S. look insignificant. The concept of jungle clearing did not prevent ambushes to any appreciable degree, but nevertheless, millions of dollars and countless hours and energy were invested in this fruitless program.

This concept was environmentally destructive as well as ill thought out. The troops said we should just pave the whole place and get it over with. They may have been right. Nevertheless, I thought again of how misdirected our war effort seemed to be, with the huge base camps like Bien Hoa, which were small American cities with shopping centers called post exchanges and the trappings of the idle military—painted rocks. It seemed almost bizarre and out of place, not to mention out of touch with reality. If we had enough men to paint rocks and enough materiel to build small cities, why could all this not be applied to the war effort if we were seriously going to challenge the communists? Our military system could not really communicate from the lower echelons to the upper; that is, from an infantry captain to a general. This stratified communications system would have serious implications when the problems could only be detected and rationally analyzed apparently only at the lower end. Our senior headquarters were simply not up to the task at hand.

Another typically American program was also in progress. We had no idea what the aircraft were spraying, but we did see them fly over us from time to time, mostly in the jungle. The aircraft were the big four-engine C-130s with wing tanks. We did not see the results until later, when the defoliant had run its course. It was another program to win the war, defoliating the jungle. This was simply preposterous: didn't the French have a worse guerrilla problem in Algeria? There was no jungle there. The U.S. seemed incapable of understanding that this was a political war. The number of leaves had nothing to do with it. We were winning the tactical battles on the ground. We were killing many more enemy than they were inflicting casualties on us, but this was not where the issue would be decided. It was a war of ideas, and we offered none or at least made the case so poorly that it was not attractive enough. We were trying to defoliate, while at night, the Vietcong came to villages and indoctrinated. We cleared the jungle, and the communists promised the farmers peace and their own land. We were simply fighting; they had a clear-cut idea of what they wanted from this war.

The average infantryman just wanted to get the job (his time) over with, and none could see how such ill-conceived programs would help in that regard. Most of us wanted more combat units to share the load; others simply counted out the days and never thought about the larger issues. However, to a man, they could smell out a lie or stupidity instantly. Political leaders in Washington and elsewhere may voice unfounded remarks about the intelligence of the infantry, but in a draftee army, they simply reflect the American public. No politician should ever try to lie to the military. Once one is in a war, the truth is an essential item. Save propaganda for the enemy. President Johnson would have been far better off telling the truth, and in return, he would have gotten the respect of his fighting men rather than their contempt. When you know you are being lied to, however well meaning, it does not help or motivate you to fight better or to die for your cause.

The crescendo of protests growing louder in the U.S. was taking a toll on all of us. I could feel it. Troops did not like to admit that they were bothered by it, but we all were, and we all sensed that something was not going well back home. It was harder to do our job. I understood what each side was saying, and there was some truth for everyone and for all sides. The protests chipped away at us in a strange sort of way, but our problems were more immediate. Many had a simple attitude of resignation about the protests. After all, what could we do about it? *We had to live through the day.*

Our concerns were the immediate ones, narrow, simple enough, and evident, not geopolitical. We wanted to get ammunition resupply tonight! *That* was important. Men argued over which C ration they would get (you were handed the next one out of the twelve-meal box when you went through the chow line), who had been on patrol the most, who got to go back to a base camp, who had to stay up all night on mortar watch or patrol, but all of us counted the days and hours we had left to serve in Vietnam, hoped we would see the sun tomorrow, and thought about the flight home and the reception we would get from our loved ones.

I had a long philosophical chat with the battalion operations officer who would later be killed, and we spoke about the New Year a few weeks away. He was a marvelous man with an infectious grin and a wry sense of humor. His helmet never seemed to fit, giving him the appearance of a new recruit, even though he was a major. A few weeks seemed so long and so far into the future that we simply could not focus on something out of our immediate range. We tried to talk about what we would be doing in a year or even two, and it was hard to envision such abstractions. They seemed so unreal and irrelevant to our current situation. Our vision was only a few hours or a day or two away at best. Where we had to go the next day and what we had to do there were more important and soaked up our thoughts.

CHAPTER 17

A DAY IN VIETNAM

Patrols had been posted the night before as usual. It was early morning, and we were on an operation in the Tay Ninh region. Our patrols went out several miles from the battalion base, but some remained closer to our base. Each patrol had a pattern and a mission, some requiring hours, others all night. Fortunately, there was no contact, only a few sounds of enemy movement, but not toward us or in any menacing manner. It was a relatively quiet time, good for training new men and helping us examine what we could do better in the future. Any day you didn't have to fight in Vietnam was a good day, one day closer to going home.

It was just before dawn when our patrols all came in. At the first sign of light, we were up, in positions, and ready for anything. Three companies arranged in a lazy circle called leaguer—probably from the South African term for when they circled their wagons in the days of the Zulu wars. We prepared for day as we did every day, with a full complement of the deadly paraphernalia of war—machine guns, automatic weapons, grenade launchers, hand grenades, smoke grenades, pistols, mortars, and the artillery forward observation party. At the officers' staff meeting, we were briefed on our mission, planned what route and tactics we would use on our operations that day, and arranged for helicopters to bring out our supplies, especially ammunition, food, and mail, when we reached our destination. We would change radio batteries, check with our artillery support to make sure that they were in range to fire if necessary, and to make advanced or prearranged fire plans should we need them, bury our unused rations, check our position, and make sure we left nothing for the enemy.

The tremendously efficient U.S. killing machine was in place and waiting. Soon it would be on the prowl and in search of prey.

First light in the morning was a particularly vulnerable time for us since we were always in unknown territory. Enemy units preferred to attack at that time, with the sun in our eyes if possible. After an hour or so, everyone had shaved, heeded the call of nature, and completed gearing up for the day. We would eat in relays: every other man ate, then the others got their turn, so not too many were preoccupied and without weapons at the ready. I was always amazed at how getting ready for a day of war was not all that different from getting ready for work in a normal business routine back home.

I had never been much of a coffee drinker but soon became one, and as soldiers will do, we developed a little ritual. Our C rations had powdered coffee, sugar, and cream. You could use an empty C ration fruit can (most of us saved a can of fruit for breakfast) as your coffee cup since it was just about the right size. All was well, except we had no routine source of heat, no large fires, and we almost never got heat pellets, little waxlike things you could light that would burn without smoke almost like a solid piece of Sterno.

Infantrymen, ingenious as ever, quickly devised a way to heat coffee, one that would horrify taxpayers since it involved the destruction of a weapon—the claymore mine. A claymore mine had a hundred or so steel balls in a plastic tray about ten to twelve inches long and five or so inches high. It had a slight frontal curve, which was to be pointed toward the enemy, and a crude sight. Composition C-4 explosive was packed behind the steel balls, and when detonated, they would spray forward, killing those unfortunates in the way.

Well, we would strip the stainless-steel ball bearings from the front of a claymore mine, break them, up and throw them around so Charlie could not use them for any purpose. Then we'd pull out the C-4 explosive from the back of the case. Once out of its plastic mine case, we would roll the C-4 (plastic explosive) into a thin, long string, usually about a foot or so in length. After this was done, you could light one end of the explosive, and it would burn—a very hot burn—but no explosion (getting this just right took some serious experimentation). As the explosive burned, we would move our cups along the hottest portion of the fire, and by the time the explosive burned out, the water was more than hot enough for coffee. A few months later, we started getting one-pound blocks of C-4 explosive, I think due to the unusual number of claymore mines that were being used. Someone had finally figured out what was happening. Since C-4 explosive came in a large cheeselike block and worked just like the explosive from a claymore mine, we switched readily. In fact, the blocks of C-4 were also useful for blowing down trees when we needed to make a helicopter landing zone in the jungle and destroying enemy bunkers. In time, we found numerous other chores for this unique war play toy.

A few weeks earlier, I had been in Cu Chi for an officers' meeting, and a lecturer spoke about the cost of weapons. I found out that the claymore mine cost about $250. We worked out the arithmetic and calculated that each cup of coffee cost about $25. Later, when I was briefing the company on this and other things, several troops gleefully indulged in additional expensive cups of coffee.

Coffee was not only expensive, but as a diuretic, it could test one's bladder to the limits. I once had two or three cups of coffee early one morning at Tay Ninh airfield and then got in a Huey observation helicopter, not thinking about how long we would be in the air. We were on an aerial observation mission, and they could last up to four or five hours, and there was no real reason to land. An hour to two later, under intense bladder pressure, I leaned out the helicopter as far as possible, with a waist strap on for safety, and tried to relieve the pressure.

Unfortunately, this helicopter did not have a piss tube that you could urinate in like some of the small fixed-wing aircraft. Backwash from the blades took the urine stream (now small droplets) right into the door-gunner's compartment. Realizing he was being pissed on, but his screams were going unheeded, the door gunner opened fire with his belt-fed M60 machine gun. Firing attracted everyone's attention, including mine. With only a fraction of the pressure gone, I stopped, got back inside, and tried to think of how to explain this to the gunner.

When we landed, I gave up and decided to simply pull rank. He was not a happy soldier. It was one thing to be in Vietnam, quite another to be in Vietnam and get pissed on, especially by an officer.

Our battalion moved out at about 8:00 am the next day. Our destination was a heavily wooded area about ten miles away. The woods were old, with very tall stately mahogany trees, the famous triple canopy of jungle growth, but there was little evidence of Charlie. A few old booby traps, some visible punji pits (their former camouflage cover had rotted away), but nothing new. They were dense, heavy woods with the exotic smells of rotting jungle and even some of the sounds. God, it was hot. The temperature must have been one hundred with the humidity not far behind. Sweat poured off everyone. The rains came by 11:00 am, and we were all soaked, collectively miserable, and in foul temper. The impact of being wet from rain (you don't dry for a long time in areas with high humidity and the rain and sweat mix) is hard to relate, but it increased our misery level perceptibly. Web gear straps, which held the things we carried, cut into shoulders deeper, feet hurt more, and uniforms lubricated by the rain seemed to be made out of wool. Absolute misery compounded by the threat of danger was our lot on days such as this.

We were, by now, lean and mean. No one fell out due to the heat, long marches, or general misery. Seasoned troops.

During the march to our new area, in the early afternoon, we stopped and waited for our routine helicopter resupply. Three helicopters flew in, carrying C rations and ammunition, known to the troops as beans and brass. When new, bullets had a shiny brass look but quickly got tarnished if not used. We seemed to have a lot of new shiny bullets. Beans and brass were the items of survival, but it was the mail from home that was precious and cherished. Mail or lack of any could and did make an enormous difference in the mental health of us all. You could tell who did or did not get mail; it made that much difference. Sometimes you could tell if the news from home was particularly good or bad. One could but wonder if people back home had any idea of how important mail could be to those of us in Vietnam.

The helicopters were big noisy birds swooping out of the air; they signaled to all who were watching exactly where you were. The helicopters usually alerted Charlie if he was around, and the VC enjoyed shelling us with mortars even more if they had the chance to bag a helicopter at the same time. Once in a while, on a good day for some soldier, his time in Vietnam would be up, and he would get on that big magnificent helicopter, with only a few handshakes from those of us who would remain. The lucky soldier would be headed home, a short flight to a base camp, then to Saigon or Bien Hoa for processing and the flight home on a big jet.

Everyone felt joy when some lucky guy left. Joy with a high dose of envy. There was almost a universal feeling of "I hope my day comes soon, and I'll be able to get on a chopper." We'd all seen the body bags being tossed on, and that was the other way to leave.

We unloaded the helicopters quickly, and each man took what he needed. With haste, the helicopters took off and were soon moving again. Each man would eat his C rations as we walked along. Everyone was quiet, cautious. Rifle safeties came off; grenade pins were partially straightened. There was more tension than usual, and it was all around and as thick as a New England fog, especially after the helicopters had left such a signal proclaiming exactly where we were. There is an old saying that "you always have the chance to be a martyr for your country." We knew that any moment could bring the sharp crack of rifle fire, and we would have our chance.

On days like this, I tried to imagine what it must have been like in World War II, being in England for months, then only in combat for relatively brief periods of time. The same was true in the Civil War, when Southern soldiers went home to plant and winter, with most of the major campaigns being fought in the spring and summer.

We got into our position for the night at about 6:00 pm, and it was already getting dark, as it did in heavy jungle. There was no chance to dig in well, we were in for big trouble and lots of casualties if Charlie had followed us and decided to attack. Shrapnel flies across the ground like bullets, but if most of your body is below ground level, your chances of being hit are reduced. After the company commanders met with the battalion commander, it was far too late to dig a position. Luckily, Steve, who was my radio-telephone operator, had dug a foxhole for me, just in case we came under fire. Some guys stayed up most of the night, preparing positions. They would be more fatigued than usual the next day and less effective on patrol but safer during the night, a trade off. But all was quiet. We put out listening posts, half a kilometer from the unit, and a couple of roving patrols. Still, nothing was reported; nothing disturbed us.

It rained again that night, and it was one of the few times I felt cold. We heard an elephant, at least I hoped it was an elephant, way off in the distance, toward the Cambodian border. An elephant would probably not live long near any area where there was combat. With all the air strikes, artillery available, and the fact that both sides would fire at sounds, a large pachyderm would attract far too much attention to go unnoticed. Even one single small mortar round going off near an elephant would shred the beast.

Oddly, our time no longer had the normal distinctions; it was simply a haze, a blur marked only by events. The normal conventions of day and month had no meaning for us. Our lives were by the hour, by dawn, dark and sun. We became experts in lunar cycles and developed the skills to determine when there would be enough light for fighting. You could get killed just as easily on Sunday as on Monday, so the day of the week or date of the month had little relevance for us. We simply plodded along, one foot in front of the other, concerned about the next hour, the next event that may cost us our lives.

It had been an average day on an average sweep or search and destroy operation by the American Army in Vietnam. Most of our days were like that, enervating, tiring, frustrating, and dangerous. Even though there was no fighting, we felt the excruciating anxiety from moment to moment almost like droplets of sweat rolling down your back; the potential was always there for instant death. We did not know there would be no fighting. The war had a deep personal impact on everyone of us. In the infantry, none of us could ever completely relax; danger was always near. We all knew that we could become a casualty figure without any warning, cause, or reason. The level of emotional strain was palpable. It sapped our energy; it was our albatross. Years later, this strain—embedded in the minds of those who served their country—would continue to corrode like rust at the soul of many a soldier who had walked in the jungles and rice paddies of Vietnam. Psychiatrists probably would have a name for it, Post traumatic stress Disorder (PTSD) or something. We did not know the extent of the impact on some soldiers at the time, but it left deep festering scars in many. For now, though, today, every man marked off one more day on his personal calendar. One less day to go in Vietnam, one more day closer to home, closer to returning to family.

Then comes the night, and with it is cover for the enemy who fears our air force and makes his moves under the cover of darkness. Night limited what we could do more than what the enemy could do. We had to rest sometimes, and since the enemy could attack at his leisure, he could rest and then attack. Night was often his choice, rarely ours. Things don't work as well at night. Men get disoriented, command is much harder, and coordination of fires more difficult. Fire coordination was critical for us. This meant getting the artillery right and on the enemy—not short rounds on us or ineffectively elsewhere. It also meant getting the air strikes right, and aircraft could not fly through incoming artillery since it could hit them. We also had to coordinate our own mortars, if we had them. All in all, a rather large task. Charlie preferred night fighting since it limited the air force and the army gunships, cutting our firepower edge significantly.

CHAPTER 18

SLAUGHTER AT SOUI TRE

President Johnson, the man who said Asian wars were for Asian boys, was at Wake Island for a major conference with military and political leaders about the direction of the war. Clearly, and with good reason, he was not happy with the way the war was going. In the military, we knew there would be calls for more U.S. troops, and the war was probably going to get worse or at least larger. Too bad a president can never descend to the level of a common infantryman; we could have told him some things that would have made a significant impact. Senior leaders are always shielded from people who know the truth. Perhaps once on a course their ego sets in, but for whatever reason, it is a serious weakness and even more so because most believe they are getting the right answers and unfiltered truth.

My battalion was now operating close to the Cambodian border in a *very* dangerous territory near a place called Soui Tre. We were part of a larger American sweep operation along the Cambodian border, which was attempting to cut the Ho Chi Mihn trail and destroy the enemy units in the area. By destroying the enemy here, we were supposed to be denying him sanctuary in Laos and Cambodia, a concept that made no sense to us at all since we were just coming close to those countries, and enemy could still operate freely in them.

We saw those people often, just fleeting glances. They were not interested in fighting—a peculiar and unusual turn of events for the aggressive Charlies. Our patrols heard them moving about a lot at night. Enemy troops must have been wondering and thinking, *Why are the Americans trying to commit suicide here?* We were so near the Ho Chi Minh trail that major enemy units could be brought up against us rapidly and with little warning. These could be big units, regiments, or even a division or two. Whatever they decided to throw at us, it would be different and probably would be from the North Vietnamese Army, regulars with full equipment and training. A lot different from Charlie, requiring a different type of tactics for us.

We had been in a position for two days when another American infantry battalion came into our leaguer, and we built berms, real dirt mounds that offered a good deal of protection. After some days, there were two infantry battalions and an artillery battalion in this one position, probably some 3,500 men. The firepower we had at our disposal was awesome, and it appeared unlikely that any North Vietnamese units, except in huge numbers, could expect to do anything against us.

Around our fifth day in the leaguer, at about 9:30 am, I was in the battalion operations center, talking to some of the other officers in our unit when our entire position was rocked by the most intense mortar and rocket bombardment I had experienced thus far in Vietnam. Five, six, seven hundred heavy explosions rumbled through our positions, numbing our ability to hear and filling the air with dust and smoke. Then it was quiet, and we knew Charlie or his North Vietnamese regulars were on their way. I frantically rushed back to my company in the moments before the coming infantry assault, not knowing if we had been dealt a savage blow by the mortars or not. Luckily, we had only four men wounded, and most of the mortars hit elsewhere in our position, which was a fairly large area.

As the smoke cleared, you could see a mile. The underbrush did not grow well in this area, but there were a few tall mahogany trees. Every unit had plenty of men on the berms in their sectors of responsibility, waiting for what we knew must come—a determined infantry assault in the true Russian style. A light wind had completely cleared the air, enabling us to see what our tormentors were doing. Meanwhile, the few wounded were already being taken care of and moved to safety since helicopter evacuation did not appear to be possible anytime soon. More ammunition was being rushed up to the berm, and every able soldier was in position.

In the previous months in Vietnam, I had rarely seen more than a few enemy troops at any one time and then on their terms. However, this time, it was to be different. In the distance we saw them: they had formed up, row after row, in what I learned later was a Soviet-style assault formation. To me, they looked like the British at New Orleans. But my fighting blood was up. We could deal with this. They were playing our game, trying to fight us on our terms. I could see their bayonets and called to my company and anyone else within earshot to fix bayonets—a loud, deep, roaring cheer went up from 3,500 Americans! All our blood was up. For all of us, after the long weeks and months of fighting an elusive enemy, he was now presenting himself to us in an astonishing array of targets. Let us all go over that goddamn berm and fight those people. The impulse to go out and do battle at close quarter was strong, but cooler heads prevailed, and we waited and waited.

Mortar shells started slamming into our position to keep us pinned down as the enemy neared. Their first assault elements were now a football field away. Many enemy troops appeared to be carrying engineering equipment, probably Bangalore torpedoes, to breech our berm. The commander of the leaguer, a full colonel, ordered us to open fire, and we did before he finished saying the word, unleashing a torrent of hot steel, explosives, and death.

The industrial firepower of the U.S. Army was in its full fury. Artillery pieces had been pulled up to the berm, firing beehive rounds as fast as they could. These were artillery shells made up of 1,500 or so small steel darts, a technological refinement of grapeshot that pinned enemy soldiers to trees and nailed their rifles to their chests. Machine guns and assault rifles fired fully automatic in a cacophony of the devil's roar.

They came from two sides; our comrades on our left were heavily engaged as well. I saw the enemy troops getting closer, but gaps were being torn in their ranks. They were all in uniform—regulars from North Vietnam as we had suspected. Americans began to fall. Enemy mortar rounds were still coming into our positions. Dust and smoke were thick, making it hard to see; the proximity to death was close and alarming.

All of a sudden, a bullet scorched through the front and exited out the left side of my fatigue jacket, just under my left arm. That, I thought, is about as close as it gets. I could hear the peculiar whine shrapnel makes as it flies through the air on its life-taking missions. The noise was incredible, and no one could hear an order if they wanted to, but we did not need orders. We were on autopilot. My company and the one to my right were the area the enemy planned to break through. *The arrogant bastards. They're coming through over our dead bodies. Of course, that was exactly what they had in mind. Fuck it. We may as well get it over with here, deal with it now.*

There were several thousand of them as near as we could tell. Probably at least three regiments. The enemy commander thought he had damaged us badly enough to move into the next phase of the battle. The enemy then committed their reserve force, and we began to feel the pressure, like an irresistible tidal wave. The ultimate outcome was never in doubt or even close, and soon, actually within minutes, the air force was overhead with a vengeance, dropping its variety of bombs, rockets, and whatever they had hung on their aircraft. Then as suddenly as it began, the enemy fire slackened, and we sensed that they were about to quit. Their attack had lost its steam due to dreadful casualties. The artillery fire kept up a steady drumbeat, and air strikes continued. I could only wonder how those people from North Vietnam could stand that type of punishment.

Our artillery and other firing ceased, and as the air force departed, scattered small arms firing was still going on. We could no longer resist the urge to meet them—meet our elusive enemy—head-on, and with one loud scream and no one in control, we went over the top of our berm to get at those people. I started running with everyone else when it dawned on me that I could not remember if my pistol was loaded or not. *Fuck.* I refused to be killed because of an empty gun, so I picked up one of their guns, an AK-47 with a full clip and bayonet. Outside our berm and protected area, here we were on the move, looking for enemy and wanting to kill them. It was time to kill the bastards, time to win the war.

Only a few broken North Vietnamese units and a rearguard were still in their places, and the men in them appeared dazed and hesitant. They were cut down with little effort. Gradually, the hazy air cleared, and the firing stopped completely. As things settled down and we began to get a grip on ourselves and the situation, we sent out a flying squad. This group of rough and tumble folks found the mortar crews that had been giving us hell. We located the firing positions, and there they were—three mortars, each with a three-man crew and a couple of other soldiers, probably ammunition porters.

The crews were just about to pack up and flee, but instead, they were killed to a man, and their mortars were now our prizes of war. It was stupid for Charlie not to protect his guns and get them out earlier. I think the air force must have destroyed their command elements, and they were surprised by the more aggressive than normal reaction of the Americans. We lugged the mortars, baseplates, and ammunition back to our positions, and groups of men went out and picked up all the weapons and ammunition scattered all over the battlefield. Weapons and ammo were precious to Charlie, but to the North Vietnamese, they appeared to have nominal value. Clearly, the nature of the war was changing.

I started counting bodies on the ground to get an idea of what we had done. My watch said the actual fighting lasted about thirty-five minutes. I could see over two hundred dead from where I was standing and could tell there were many more around. Twenty-seven Americans were killed.

A final count of enemy dead yielded over 1,100. I looked at them: small, young, skinny, and dead. They never had a chance; they could not fight us on our terms. To me, their attack was patent stupidity, probably an order from someone at a desk far away. But their leaders wanted to embarrass President Johnson, and they were prepared to make serious sacrifices. So they came, wave after suicidal wave. It was obvious that their side made plenty of mistakes too, and this one was costly and achieved absolutely nothing.

Secretary of defense McNamara had developed a method of quantifying the war known as body counts. This grotesque statistical quantification of death was as outrageous in its conception as in its effect on the men who had to do it. After any engagement, no matter how large or small, we had to accurately account for all enemy casualties. It took only a brief period of time for the enemy to determine what we were up to. They then began to ambush U.S. troops sent out to count bodies. We began to counterambush, and the process degenerated into a macabre, deadly exchange over the dead. Counting enemy dead became a game, and few of us were willing to risk our lives to aid McNamara's accountants calculate some inane actuarial conclusion about the war. In a way, it was a ghoulish activity and cheapened us even in our own eyes. Body counting—even the name was denigrating—also made you literally come face-to-face with the consequences of war, and they are in no way pleasant.

There were other problems with this body-count business that went somewhat deeper. Men engaged in warfare for their country do not like indications that they are being reduced to statistics and meaningless bureaucratic numbers. We knew we were cogs in some misguided machinery, but to have it rubbed in your face was something else. It had a stultifying effect and dug out another unspoken notch in our collective morale.

As I walked through the carnage of this bloody engagement, my fighting blood long ebbed, I could see that the firing had been so intense that even brush and small trees were cut down almost at ground level. A few hours later, a giant crane helicopter came in carrying a small bulldozer. The dozer was sent to dig a pit for the bodies. After the pit was dug, I looked in at row after row of mangled bodies and could not help but think, *My god, are we Nazis?* Even though the slaughter had been merciless, at least they were soldiers in uniform, armed and prepared to do what they had been ordered to do. No, after all that could and would be said and done, we were not Nazis.

After Soui Tre, I could not eat for two days, and my weight dwindled to below 150 pounds. A lot of generals came out from Saigon, had their pictures taken with the troops, and told us what a good job we had done. It was for the press, but I found those types of activities depressing. I could take no pride in this business. I thought of the patriotism that inspired me to volunteer for combat and the expectations of carrying the banner of freedom against communism that I carried in my mind when I got to this place. Now we were burning villages, killing people in vast numbers, spending our national wealth, and tearing up a country in Asia, and none of us had the slightest idea why we were doing this or what it was supposed to achieve. The pall of meaningless efforts and political malaise hung to my thoughts like ticks on a Georgia dog. Relentlessly sucking out my energy and nerves.

This particular engagement stayed with me as an exception to the rules of our war in more ways than one. Indeed, Soui Tre would stay with many of us as a pivotal point in the war. We had come face-to-face with ourselves and how the war had brutalized all of us. We now had a clearer idea of just what kind of enemy we were up against. An enemy that did not care about sacrifices as long as his political will prevailed. I overheard two soldiers talking, and one said, "We are going to have to kill every man in North Vietnam to end this stupid war." The other responded, "No, you idiot, we are going to have to kill everyone in Vietnam to win."

The stark reality was that we would have to kill most of the men in North Vietnam to win, but even more alarming is that we would have to kill many from the South as well. Then we would have to kill new generations to win because it was becoming evident that the leaders in Hanoi would fight on as long as necessary to achieve their goals. Numbers were not on our side; polarization was taking place in our own ranks, and it did not bode well for us.

CHAPTER 19

A NIGHT SPENT ON BUFFALO DUNG

We always looked for a good position to leaguer or stay overnight. We preferred high, dry ground that could be defended easily, with a place for helicopters to land. Helicopters increased our mobility significantly since we did not have to carry more than a day's supplies on a normal trek, and on major operations, they could carry us to our target. So instead of several days worth of C rations and as much ammo as you could carry, you could get by with a day's rations, but most guys did not skimp on ammunition. Each company had a box that could be picked up daily and redelivered in the evening. This frequently held our ponchos (crude raincoats and ground blanket), and other gear we would not need while moving to the next position. Sometimes the helicopters would not make it back out on the routine runs, but they usually did. It was also comforting to know that if you were wounded, the helicopters would come in to get you and take you to medical attention quickly, except under the most dire circumstances.

We had been moving through the rice paddies on an extended search and destroy mission for several days in an area southwest of Saigon. Here, the landscape dropped from the flat lightly forested cover to the inundated rice paddy sea known as the Mekong Delta. The delta did not have many American units, and most of us did not like the idea of being there. No fighting but lots of wet walking in sultry air that reminded me of the worst summer day Florida had to offer. We had trekked knee deep through swamp water, through lots of rice paddies, and through small canals. It had rained frequently. We were soaked from head to toe and had been for a couple of days. Sweat added to our moisture and misery levels. We wanted to get to dry ground so we could try to dry out before rot—the old famous trench foot—started to set in. We also could operate from a good area for a brief period of time, a day or two, three at the most. If you stayed any longer, your pattern and movements were noted by an enemy who was always alert to any small vulnerability. Once the enemy was in possession of such intelligence, it could result in ambushes, mines, traps, or even the possibility of being overrun in a full-scale assault.

We had not had the advantage and assistance of helicopter support during this operation, so we could not fly our normal aerial reconnaissance and plan our routes and night's position as well as we liked. No helicopters also meant that we had to carry all our gear and supplies. This loaded the average soldier down with at least seventy-five pounds or more.

About midafternoon on our journey, we could see a hill way off in the distance even though it was not on our maps. Not too big, but maybe big enough for our purposes. We forged ahead, and after some three hours of hard marching, with little thought of security, we got there just as darkness fell.

Our hill turned out to be an enormous mound of buffalo shit. The buffalo refuse had been collected gradually by Vietnamese farmers to spread on their fields to increase the fertility of the soil. I don't know why they had stored it in such a way, but there it was, a small mountain of buffalo dung. Most of the men chose to bed down scattered out in the rice paddies, but the battalion command group was committed to the hill of shit, the high ground. Some put ponchos on the ground, but the worms and bugs crawled over them quickly.

Few of us felt like sleeping that long and uncomfortable night. The next day would be hell for most of us.

I took the option to remain with my company, which was strung out along the rice paddy dikes in every direction. We put out some security, but it was far from adequate, just perfunctory. *Man,* I thought, *if they hit us tonight, there will be hell to pay.* We did not sleep much better than the poor souls on the shit pile. When the sun came up, it was a hot, smelly, and humid day. Under such conditions, it is no wonder that soldiers are young and must be. The oldest man in our battalion was thirty-six, and he was the sergeant major. The battalion commander was only thirty-five. At twenty-six, I was called the Old Man.

After officer's call, when we started to depart from our lofty position, I could see out across surrounding areas, which looked oddly beautiful and peaceful. Some small wooded areas, a few water buffalo casually grazing, farmers here and there tending their paddies. A light breeze had picked up, probably from the ocean. For a while, it was almost cool, pastoral, and, in some ways, enticing. Startlingly clear nights, countrysides of green, and a level of agricultural harmony and tranquility probably unlike any other. I knew the picture was surreal, and that reality was something different. Again, I thought, *How little is what it appears to be in this country, where even a distant mountain on closer inspection transforms itself into a pile of shit?*

Aerial reconnaissance was normally part of our daily routine, so small unit commanders could see where we were headed and make plans and provisions for any unusual situations. After two days without this luxury, we had our helicopter friends back. On this particular day, I went with the battalion commander, airborne in a Huey observation helicopter for several hours. On other flights, I had noticed that I could see enemy positions with little trouble and that others could sometimes not see at all, even when they were being destroyed by artillery fire. The unit was moving only a few miles, and we had no contact or emergencies, so I thought it would be a good time to investigate this peculiarity, which enabled me to see what others could not. Since I had already spotted a bunker-type position, the scene was set. The helicopter circled for some time over the bunker, and I tried repeatedly to point it out, but no one else could see it, so I called in artillery fire myself and destroyed it all the same. I had discriminated what others could not. I had had some artillery training and was used to their techniques, plus my forward observer had given me some excellent lessons. Later the same day, we saw another structure. Same experience: I could see it; the others could not.

Being color blind with poor definition of red and green, it did not occur to me that this could ever be an asset. We reported this phenomenon, and sometime later, the brigade commander went up with me to investigate this happening. The results were the same, and he reported his observations to division headquarters. I spoke with the division commander, and we went up as well but did not find any targets to display my physical handicap. Later we received a division regulation stating that about one-third of the aerial observers *should* be color blind. Other units had reported similar findings. A color-blind person apparently has better definition for texture, perhaps nature's way of compensating for the weakness in color. This meant color-blind observers could see enemy fortifications and positions that may have been missed by others since camouflage is normally done for color and getting the texture/harmony right would be much harder.

It was refreshing to see the military react and adapt to use such clever approaches when appropriate. My admiration for the army's quick reaction was soon dashed upon discovering that using color-blind observers had been a technique used in World War II. Apparently, it had been a hard-learned lesson then, and the army had not preserved this body of knowledge. Useful tactics seemed to be disregarded as soon as possible, only to be rediscovered and rebuilt at a high cost in effort and lives.

CHAPTER 20

IN A FOXHOLE FULL OF WATER

After the infamous buffalo-shit-mountain episode, we did not have any contact or fighting for just over a week. This was always a relief because it gave us some time to collect our wits and to operate at something less than a breakneck pace. We then moved back to more familiar ground, between War Zones C and D. The area was known as a very dangerous region, fairly low and often wet. After we had been there for almost a week, we began skirmishing for several days. Our repeated attempts to catch an elusive force of Charlies failed. We had killed a few of the enemy, but done nothing to seriously damage any of their units. This was a deadly game of cat and mouse. Funny, one never thinks of being the mouse, always the cat. Here it was a toss-up and could change at a moment's notice.

After another day of humping the boonies (walking in large company-sized patrols through the bush), we got to our night position too late to dig in properly. The area we had to leaguer in was low and covered with scrub. The tall mahogany trees had been taken out by a timber crew years before. The monsoon had started and was now in full swing, so it rained a lot every day. When we started to dig a foxhole, it would immediately fill with water. One shovel full of dirt out, one shovel full of water right back in. You could not really dig a full bunker or a fighting foxhole, but if you got a hole or pit large enough to crouch in, it could give you some limited protection. I hated to step in mud that went over the top of my boots since wet feet meant sore feet, especially if mud got mixed in with socks and skin. Sometimes it was hard to get the time or place where you could dry your boots, socks, and feet out completely, making it all the worse. Our boots had canvas sides, and water would seep in at the ankle level or higher, but there was something worse about mud coming in from the top of the boot. Getting in mud, or at least muddy water up to your neck, was simply no fun at all. We were pretty grim people and collectively about as irritable as humans could be.

We had sent out patrols as usual. Things like this became so ordinary in combat that we simply didn't have to think about them. We had gotten a lot of replacements during the past three weeks, and they badly needed additional training. One of the new sergeants took out his first patrol. Perhaps it was bad luck or just inexperience, but he got disoriented in the bush. Instead of heading straight out for some three miles and setting up a listening post, he accidentally made a lazy circle and eventually came back in the direction of the unit.

Later we discovered that he had gone on dead reckoning rather than using his compass—a bad mistake, especially in areas where visibility was so limited. When the green sergeant on patrol heard some noise, thinking it was an enemy unit, he (and the rest of his patrol) began to fire 40-millimeter grenades (from the M79 grenade launcher—our answer to the RPG) into our positions. The first one landed about twenty feet from me, with a sharp sickening crack. I flew in to my water hole, and the rest of my valiant little band followed instantly in to their own syrupy holes. *Shit.*

Of course, we thought initially that this was mortar fire was from Charlie and returned fire as best we could. Three men went down wounded before we could sort the whole thing out and stop the firing. Once engaged in combat, even against your own and when it is a dreadful mistake—and it is very difficult to get the situation under control. You fired at sounds much of the time, along with movement when detected and generally where you think the enemy is. Smoke, haze, darkness, screams, and noise frequently made combinations that complicated matters beyond belief.

Our medics went into action to save the three wounded men now demanding attention. The medevac helicopters were on the scene within fifteen or twenty minutes and the wounded men out and on their way to better medical care. The brilliant color of blood, especially during a rain and in the mud, illuminated with flashlights was striking to me that night. The only good news was that those wounded would all survive, and none of the wounds were too serious. Serious wounds were those that took eyesight, limbs, genitals, face, or caused brain damage. Even with that somewhat rosy prognosis, I knew it was simply a case of more American men wounded, their lives altered forever in this strange land.

I had noticed for some time and mentioned to the battalion commander during officers call or just when I had a moment or two alone with him, the questionable quality of replacements, especially the level of their training. One company had recently gotten several new replacement soldiers who, during their training in the U.S., had fired only five bullets from the M16 rifle, our basic weapon. New sergeants were being turned out of training centers for noncommissioned officers (noncoms) too fast in a process called shake and bake. Some of the older personnel in the regular army were out of shape physically and could not stand the grueling pace of infantry service in Vietnam. The replacements we were getting were too young and inexperienced, but at least most seemed to be able to handle the physical side. This type of situation may well be true in all wars, but the results for the Americans in Vietnam were higher casualties and serious problems with morale.

All of war is not experience, seasoning, and being in physical condition. Morale is the elixir of battle. To do this terrible thing, men need to be psychologically prepared to kill. Society teaches us not to do that, but war makes it a necessity. The hardest part is teaching young men and having them believe that the cause they are fighting for is worth sacrificing their lives if need be. Morale is that basic underpinning of a military machine that gives it flair, daring, and an appetite to get at the enemy. Without it, a military organization will be sluggish, shy, and make mistakes. Its execution of orders will be poor, and it will have no sharp edge to its sword.

Later that night, we came under fire again. Somehow I just could not get back into that water-filled hole. *Screw it*, I thought, *if I'm going to get it, it won't be in a goddamn water hole in the ground.* I simply stretched out on the ground on my stomach and kept the radio handset at my ear to coordinate our reaction. Afterward, when patrols had chased away whoever was harassing us, I thought about my feelings again. I could tell then that care for my physical well being was slipping—it did not seem to matter much what happened to me anymore. I knew that this was wrong, that my grip on my psyche was edging away. I knew this even as I recognized that my sanity depended on my clinging to my responsibilities as an officer and adherence to the credo of duty, country, honor, and the things dear to me. These were my remaining underpinnings, but my psyche was battered, my resolve undermined.

By this time, my body was in full-scale revolt. Diarrhea was a constant reminder of our plight, but it seemed to be getting worse. My radio operator now had to open my C rations. I thought if I could just control my hands, which continued to tremble much of the time, I'd be in fairly good shape. But the growing malady was deeper and more resonant. It dawned on me that my personal situation was, in some small way, a partial reflection of what America was going through. We all wanted to do the right thing, but we knew intuitively that what was going on was wrong, and it was having a devastating national effect.

That same night, unable to sleep under the circumstances, I spoke to our medic, a married man with two children. He was a conscientious objector who had elected to serve as a medic. (One could never fault the courage of medics.) He told me of his fear of death and how he knew he would die and soon. I assured him most of us had fears similar to his and that it did not mean that such dire predictions would be realized. I asked him to tell me why he had the feeling he would die. He said that when he heard the cry for a medic, he would always get up and go to that man, no matter what, and with the heavy fighting we had been in, he felt his luck was running out. He said he had experienced dreams in which he stood up and was blown to bits by huge cannons while Charlie looked on and laughed. He told me time and again that he did not want to die.

My attempts to convince him that we were all going to be okay and that he too would live seemed to stick a bit. After a while, he became a little more optimistic, and we ended our conversation. While I could not seem to control my situation to the degree I wished, at least I'd helped to put this medic's mind at ease.

A few months later, on a bright wake-up day for this young medic, I had the distinct pleasure of shaking his hand as he boarded a helicopter and flew out, headed for home. His premonitions had not come true; he had survived and was going home to his wife. For him, it was a good ending.

CHAPTER 21

THE LOOK OF DEATH

It was that brief look on his face the instant I shot him—that momentary fleeting look of surprise and fear as death embraced his soul.

The tidal wave of enemy troops had crested our position—they had broken through, every infantryman's ultimate nightmare. When the fighting gets in this close, we would be firing in all directions. Command and control would be lost; the artillery and air strikes could not assist us. Our advantages in firepower would be minimized, leaving us, enemy and friend alike, in little clusters of men struggling against one another, every man for himself. The lowest rung in Dante's *Inferno*—hand-to-hand combat—was now upon us.

We had heard them coming, and I could see their bayonets gleaming in near-straight rows in the false moonlight of flares being fired by our artillery, which was stationed miles away. The flares fired by the 155 mm artillery pieces would hang in the air for several minutes, and the artillerymen had worked out the technique of firing them so that one or two were constantly overhead, illuminating the jungle when we needed it. The jungle we were in was thick and intense. We had come to this place, up close to the border with Laos, in driblets, a few at a time on individual helicopters. The North Vietnamese probably thought we were a much smaller force, possibly just a company instead of a battalion (they were right to some degree since we were under strength and missing one company). This meant that we had only three companies, battalion headquarters, and a small detachment of artillerymen and one heavy weapons section, just over six hundred men in all. Enemy reconnaissance had been poor; they were not so good in the jungle because most of the North Vietnamese regulars were urban types from Hanoi and Haiphong. When they attacked, it was without fanfare, just a few mortar shells and then an unsophisticated ground assault. To them, they probably thought this was a simple matter, crushing an American company. I could see them coming at us, and we began to fire, and I also saw some of them fall as they were hit. They were not really people, just objects to fire at.

They fought their way in close, especially against the company next to mine. Each company formed a third of a circle, with battalion headquarters and the artillerymen being the only reserve force and located in the center of our circle. Confusion was supreme. The enemy believed and was correct to some degree that darkness nullified some of our advantages, particularly in aircraft. At night, when the first shots are fired, you are temporarily deaf due to the overwhelming decibel level of weapons. Weapons firing, flares, and explosions all cause blooming in your eyes, like looking at a lightbulb when it comes on in a dark room, so you are also temporarily blind. So the resulting effect was that in a small jungle area, we had over six hundred temporarily blind, deaf men firing weapons and trying like hell to stay alive, being assaulted by hundreds more who are probably even more terrified at what they had to face.

I could tell by the sounds that enemy troops were getting inside our perimeter. I got up to go to battalion headquarters to see if an emergency reaction force was needed to push the enemy troops out. My company had a platoon in reserve, and this was larger and more capable than the small battalion/artillery reserve force. As I turned, a strange uniform was before me. Luckily, I had my Colt .45 pistol cocked and ready. The .45, as everyone called it, is the standard sidearm or weapon for officers. The .45 really kills; it is a marvel of simplicity, cheap manufacturing, and lethality. It fires a large bullet at low velocity. When it hits, it is not unlike a small cannonball or the old musket ball of Revolutionary War times. I saw him and instantly recognized someone different, **an enemy uniform**, just someone that didn't look like us. Instinctively, I simply pointed and shot—a process that took less than a microsecond. I was not even sure I had hit him but then realized his body had done a complete somersault when the bullet struck his head, and he was now lying face down in the dirt, with his AK-47 assault rifle underneath him.

Heavy fighting continued for what seemed like hours until enough blood was spilled. We fired everything—artillery, mortars, rifles, machine guns, grenade launchers, and claymore mines. The air force came over time and again, striking at the enemy well outside our perimeter. The small force that had penetrated into our position, about fifty men, was killed, but they had done their damage, and our casualties were not light. We resealed our perimeter with my reserve platoon and continued to fend off probes and small groups of enemy as they moved around, seeking a soft spot in our defenses. They were like a pack of jackals circling a wounded animal, waiting to come in for the kill.

There was sporadic firing through much of the night, leaving no chance for sleep, a night in hell. Once we were sure they had retreated to their jungle lairs, we relaxed some, and the first rays of the morning sun started to appear. The sun rose, and I remembered the man I had shot only a few feet outside my humble dirt bunker position. When I saw him face down in the dirt, I kicked his body over; there was no back to his head. The bullet had entered just above the left eye. He still had some of the look I had seen fleetingly the night before. I searched his body for anything of intelligence value and found his identity card. His identity card showed he was a mere fifteen-year-old. I had killed a child, but a well-armed child.

Again, the war and what we were doing and what was being done to us struck me with its full malevolent force. *Who kills fifteen-year-olds and who sends fifteen-year-old children to die?* I knew these questions would linger in my mind for years, if I lived. The face of a fifteen-year-old soldier would be etched into the memory of my life. *Insanity.*

CHAPTER 22

JACKSON GOES DOWN

Some people are better than others at what they do or even at most things; some are more valuable contributors to humanity or just plain better in some obscure, subtle way. Maybe you just simply like them more because they earn a special place in your mind, an elusive quality, but one that is there. Boiling a description of someone down to a resume is difficult; people are hard to quantify. But Jackson was one of those exceptional people. Never saw him without a smile. Always in the thick of a fight and willing to help anyone in trouble or, when there was not trouble, just help. Jackson was always there, always around, he always made his presence felt. He was a superb artillery forward observer and an outstanding soldier. Smart, alert, and quick to do the right thing with his big guns. Always had the artillery when and where you needed it and knew all the proper techniques on how to use their fire to our maximum advantage. We used artillery to navigate sometimes since it was easy to get lost in the jungle, and Jackson could always pinpoint our location.

Jackson had also been in the unit longer than any other forward observer. So to his other talents, he could add a significant experience factor. He claimed he liked service in the infantry and was planning to switch from the artillery branch to the infantry when he returned to the U.S. Something that would not endear him to artillerymen and would only be done out of very high motivation.

When we settled in after a day's activities, he liked to sleep in a captured Charlie hammock, which he could rig up in minutes. The enemy hammock was light and small, and you could fold it up and easily put it in your leg pocket. The hammock had a cord at each end, and you could string it up between two trees and sleep off the ground, which had some advantages and some drawbacks. I cautioned him that if we came under enemy fire, especially by small mortars or RPGs, he could catch hell before he got out of the hammock and under some kind of cover. But being able to sleep off the ground and perhaps get better rest was too tempting for him.

We were on a hillside in the troubled region known as the Parrot's Beak. Not too much action during that day, but we knew Charlie was around. Some sniper fire, a few rounds of heavy machine gun fire. Not much, but it was evident that we were being stalked. Then during the darkest part of the night, between 2:00 and 3:00 am, the enemy started to fire 60-millimeter mortar rounds at us. That type of mortar was particularly bad even though it was hardly larger than a grenade. The 60-millimeter mortar did not have the typical high parabolic arc of a larger mortar round. They were almost a flat-trajectory weapon, like a rifle, and the shells came straight into your position with almost no warning. You just heard the explosions when the shell hit and detonated.

Jackson was torn from his hammock by the first round that came in. A large piece of shrapnel shredded its way through his left lung and lodged into the other lung on its swath of destruction. I could hear his screams and instantly went to his aid. Jackson had now been stretched out on the ground and was bleeding horribly. The shrapnel had entered just under his left armpit and left a gaping hole there, and blood spurted out from this point and was virtually pumping out of his mouth and nose. It did not seem that there was much left inside his lungs, even though judging from the entry hole, the piece of metal appeared to be no larger than half of a little finger. He could not breathe except for short gasps, and then he began coughing up dark-red blood. He cried, and it was clear that he was in extreme agony. The shelling stopped after five to six more rounds, and there was no further enemy action.

After seeing men wounded and killed in combat, we became somewhat expert in this type of battlefield triage. Shrapnel was particularly bad, in that it was irregular in shape, usually with sharp edges, very hot and very dangerous. The damage it could do to the human body can't be overstated. It could saw off a leg effortlessly or render a man headless like a giant sword. Shrapnel was capricious; you never knew where it was coming from or what it may do. From experience, I could tell almost immediately that Jackson's wound was going to be fatal. His upper body was torn up too badly for any other prognosis. His vital signs were failing immediately. Unfortunately, my initial impression turned out to be correct.

I tried my best to bandage him, but the wound area was seeping too much blood and did not want to accept a bandage, and I knew that it made no difference anyway. The medics took over. Jackson continued to gurgle up blood, but slower now, suggesting that his end was near, that he would die soon. Enemy mortar shells started to come into the position again. Under fire and with enemy troops near, the normally audacious medevac helicopters could not come into our position because if they did, they would simply be shot down. So Jackson lay there dying. After a few more moments, he gave a few brief body spasms as the life ebbed and bled out of him.

Grasping my semiautomatic shotgun, which was my preferred weapon of the moment, I organized a flying combat squad to knock the shit out of the mortars that had killed Jackson. Then in a vain effort, I tried to attach three grenades to my web gear. My first sergeant finally had to put them on me since I was having some difficulty managing this with trembling hands. I was in a cold fury as the fifteen-man detachment formed up. I wanted revenge. I wanted blood, and by goddamn, I was going to get it. I hoped to be able to see the mortar crew and warn them just before we cut them to pieces. It was a feeling I was having more and more with each combat loss. The bastards who did this would pay, and dearly.

Before we left our position, Jackson regained consciousness for a few minutes and asked me if he could be awarded an infantryman's decoration, the Combat Infantryman Badge. Then he choked to death on his own blood. As an artilleryman, he would not automatically be authorized the badge, but he wanted it anyway. Jackson, married just before he came to Vietnam and carrying pictures of a newly born child, was dead. His widow would get his Combat Infantryman Badge. Jackson, the best of the best, was dead.

We began sweeping through the woods near where we thought our enemy would be, but we did not find them—the mortars and their crews had fled into the night, leaving no trace that they had tormented us or where they had gone. They were good guerrillas; they had done their damage and fled quickly in true obedience to Mao Tse Tung's rules of warfare. They would live to fight another day, perhaps to kill other Americans.

We all missed Jackson immediately. Another valuable human being had been lost. I would have to write a letter to his mother and father and his wife. *What might he have contributed to our society and humanity in general? Why sacrifice this man for Vietnam?* More and more, my men asked me, "Why the hell are we here, sir? What in the hell are we doing here, Captain?" I certainly had no answers to these difficult questions. I harbored many of the same questions myself and was beginning to experience more difficulty in answering them. But I knew that American military morale was in a tailspin and that historically armies without high morale suffer needless casualties and lose wars. We had to arrest and reverse this morale issue if possible to avoid having more men die needlessly.

At the cutting edge, where infantrymen were executing American foreign policy, many of us knew that the war was not going to be won, at least certainly not as it was being envisioned back in Washington DC. Day by day, we viewed this American misadventure as collective madness and could only speculate about what our superiors were thinking. All the time, we knew our lives were in the middle, in the dangerous void between the reality of war and political fantasy. We huddled together in the hopes of staying alive. There was no cheering, no bravado, just desperate, tired, dirty men who wanted very much to live and to get home. This to me was the most sincere form of bravery. Men doing their jobs, asking only for the opportunity to get back home, alive. It was bravery in the face of isolation and futility.

My exasperation was total; I had initially wanted to win the war against communism. Now I knew that this was nothing of what I had expected. This was no national crusade, no war against a true enemy. This was just fighting for nothing. This incredible waste, this violation of humanity, this affront to what is right. This is my prayer—get us out of here any way possible, but please get us out of here. Let us go back home.

CHAPTER 23

C RATIONS AND LIFE IN THE BUSH

There were twelve basic combat or C rations, but only eight or so seemed edible as far as I was concerned. It all depended on your taste and over the long haul on what you could tolerate. For me, lima beans and ham, scrambled eggs and bacon were particularly unpalatable. Most were three to five years old, some were older, and that probably did not help the taste. All were high in protein, though, and that, according to some dietitian in the Pentagon or somewhere, is what we infantrymen needed to keep us in fighting condition.

I did like the chicken and turkey meals, and tuna was not too bad. The Cs, as we called them, did have good cake deserts in a few versions, and sometimes you would find canned fruit or some other fairly good stuff. Beenie Weenies (small cans of sliced hot dogs and baked beans) were pretty good and seemed universally popular. The bread, which came in a can, was simply inedible and was sometimes used as targets. Once in a while, someone would find a note or a special something an anonymous person back in the world who packed C rations had stuck in. It kind of made your day. These little things mean a lot when you really need them. We received almost no support from home, the world, except from our immediate families, so any hint that we had—that someone was saying thanks, that somebody actually cared—was incredibly welcomed. Some of the notes were as old as the C rations and simply said, "Hi, GI," but that did not matter at all. The light cardboard box C rations came in made excellent stationary, and I would jot down notes on a piece of this paper, cryptic but simple in style and to serve as a memory jog should I ever want to write anything about our experiences. I kept my notes inside my helmet to keep them dry as possible and would periodically send a batch home to my mother. She kept each and every one, and these notes would be most helpful to me at a later date

Troops would carry all kinds of spice and sauce to liven up the rations and vary the taste. Bottles of A1 steak sauce, dried onions, Tabasco sauce, etc., were all present in almost everyone's baggy pants pockets. The only drawback about carrying such condiments, aside from the weight, was if you got hit in the leg and some of that stuff was blown into the wound, it usually did not help. Tabasco or hot sauce could also look like blood at night, preventing a good assessment of the severity of a wound. A couple of bottles of sauce in a pocket would also rattle, something you did not need on patrol since it could alert the enemy, so troops were inspected to make sure that did not happen. We all took some chances, though, that made our lives a little easier; my personal favorite was barbecue sauce. The desire for variety and some spice won out almost universally over precaution.

The C rations and infrequent hot meals were spartan and utilitarian, not designed to be gourmet food but rather to impart enough energy for the tasks of young men at war. We usually popped Cs early in the morning before heading out into the bush. After that, we ate when we could, if we wanted to. Most did not bother until we settled in for the night somewhere. As a consequence of diet, diarrhea, and routine, we were all skinny and gaunt. Food packages from home were the most prized items a soldier could get. Universally, the recipient took a small sample and shared the rest with his comrades, his true family in this unforgiving situation. These were the only people with whom he would ever be able to truly relate, who would understand this *thing* we were in, this *experience* we were having. Sharing our food packages from home became a kind of a communion among brothers at war. Only fruitcake, ample around Christmas, would ever be rejected, and then only due to complete saturation.

Everybody carried gadgets. Swiss army knives were a useful favorite. We all had tools for cleaning and maintaining weapons, but who would think about a fingernail clipper in a combat zone? We all shared various hardware items, but there was never enough of that type of stuff. Clippers for field haircuts, tweezers to remove splinters, and other things civilized people take for granted, we all shared. Ballpoint pens, grease pens (for marking maps covered with clear plastic or acetate), string, shoelaces for boots, and a dozen other items were prized possessions. Even C rations required a can opener, and the army provided an ingenious tool, the P-38, a small finger-operated can opener that you could keep on the chain with your dog tags so as to always be able to open a C and eat when you wanted to. C rations had a sundry pack with cigarettes, gum, and other stuff many troops liked, and each C ration meal had a small packet of sugar, pepper, salt, dehydrated cream, and a little roll of toilet paper.

Personal hygiene was very hard to maintain in war, at least our kind of war. A fingernail clipper could help as could moist towelettes and dental floss. If they should ever make a realistic war movie and illustrate a bit of field sanitation, recruitment would drop off sharply. I certainly never thought of these aspects of war myself prior to experiencing them in the countryside of Vietnam. Field sanitation is very important since with over one thousand men in a position, it would get extremely unhealthy if proper latrines were not prepared and their use enforced. Since we got little plastic forks in our Cs, hand washing was not too important.

One gadget we usually carried was a smoke grenade. The color varied, but red, white, and yellow seemed to be the most popular. Whenever we were trying to mark a helicopter landing zone, we would pop smoke. Initially, we would say over the radio, "Popping yellow smoke," or whatever the color was. One day, we radioed to an incoming chopper that we had popped yellow smoke and the helicopter pilot radioed back to us that there were two yellow smokes; he wanted to know which was the right one. We had set off only one smoke grenade on the ground! Charlie, being clever, had listened to our radio communications and found out what we were doing, carried the right kind/color of grenade, and was trying to lure a helicopter into a deadly ambush.

We immediately sent out patrols to engage the enemy who were setting a trap but found nothing. Afterward, a type of code was developed in which white meant purple, yellow meant green, and so on. This could be and usually was changed daily. As soon as this new code went into effect and we saw the other incorrect color show up, we could attack the impostors with the weapons we had at hand or by calling in air strikes. Soon we had no more attempts to deceive helicopters into an ambush. We felt quite protective of helicopters since they were our lifeline. We also had great respect for the men who flew them. It took guts, frequently their missions such as resupply were not glamorous, but the work had to be done. Their casualties were among the highest of any group during the war.

On Thanksgiving Day, we were back fighting in the Michelin rubber plantation. Skirmishing would be a better way to describe what was going on, but after nine months in-country, I considered a single fired bullet as fighting. With Nui Ba Dien Mountain in the distance, with its ever-present cloud on the top, the areas looked peaceful and calm. The base camp at Dau Tieng was not too far away, so a marvelous Thanksgiving meal was prepared in one of the large kitchens in the base camp and flown out to us on helicopters in insulated containers.

Turkey, mashed potatoes, gravy, cashews, bread, pumpkin pie, the works. Great meal. It was amazing what American ingenuity and resources could do in a hostile land so far away. Essentially, the American Thanksgiving meal was being served to thousands of men located in a jungle in Asia. It was, however, far too rich in comparison to the C rations we were so used to. We were sick to a man. Everyone was vomiting like crazy, so our higher headquarters had to pull us out of active operations and let us rest for a couple of days at Dau Tieng. No one meant to make us sick, and we had all appreciated the meal. Rich, plentiful food just is not what an infantryman's diet calls for after months of being on C rations. *Next Thanksgiving would be better, especially if somehow this damn war was over.*

Smell became very important. I remember the smell of gun cleaning oil. I could smell it instantly when coming into our position, if I had been out on patrol or away for any other reason. Gun oil is a smell that will stay with me for life. Once we had our Vietnamese interpreters ask some of the Charlies we captured how they could track us so well. The answer came back that smell was their best resource. We had unscented soap, shaving cream, and anything else that we thought might smell. However, we found out that it was our high-protein diet that gave us a smell that the Vietnamese compared to wet dogs, and that is apparently how they were able to follow us so well. The smell of gunpowder, artillery smoke, helicopter exhaust, purified water, and the odor of smoke grenades were all peculiar but distinctive. Even our canvas web gear had a distinct odor, like army green, an odor one does not forget.

We would go weeks without bathing. No showers in the jungle. Your hands felt slick and gained their own coating as natural oil filled up the prints in your skin. After a few days, it seemed no one had body odor. Perhaps bacterial colonies or something else took over. Maybe we just got used to it, but we did not smell particularly bad to one another. Sweating a lot probably helped us keep clean to some degree. I remember feeling rain and thinking it was not bad as a temporary expedient shower. Most of us got large blackheads and other signs of skin irritations. Many of us had bamboo sores, those festering boil-type inflammations on our arms and the back of our necks from going through bamboo. Bamboo stalks have small almost-invisible thorns at every joint in the bamboo stalk. When we were walking through tall bamboo, we came in contact with those thorns. They became imbedded in the skin and soon produced a major irritation. In the heat and humidity, they festered, got reinfected, and soon boil-like sores appeared. Insects would swarm around us, especially at night, and their bites would also get infected. If you scratched them, the irritation would bleed and would take weeks to heal.

In short, our world was one of dirt, discomfort, filth, constant wetness, sleeplessness, grinding fatigue, and the unremitting opportunities to become a casualty. We shared this discomfort, and after the first few weeks in-country, almost no one ever mentioned it simply because it was part of our common experience, like the heat. None of us felt heroic, but we did feel it would be heroic to survive and return to the world. That was our goal.

These thoughts call to mind the subject of boredom, and the role inactivity plays in wartime. My prewar image of such things was that men were in combat most of the time, night and day. While we seemed to be on operations a lot, we were actively fighting only a small portion of the time. It was hard to quantify. Perhaps a quarter of the time or something like that. Vietnam was different in that there were no front lines, no clear distinctions. You could get killed on a quiet day while doing nothing. In Vietnam, you never had a day off, no free time, no time to relax. At least this was the case in combat units. Some combat had a distinctly routine quality about it; other times it was absolutely deadly. Sometimes there was no combat, but you could step in a punji pit or a mine and be maimed or killed without an enemy soldier for miles around. A sniper could put a bullet right in your chest or helmet, and no one else would get a scratch. Walking through the rural areas of Vietnam looking for an invisible enemy was, in fact, boring. After the novelty wore off, it assumed a monotony of its own. A dull rhythm that could lull you into accepting the natural beauty of Vietnam as nature's response to the ugliness of war. It could also play with your mind, dulling the sharpness you had to maintain and eroding the vigilance this very personal, intimate war required.

The routine was the same, and the results were the same. In a way, it contributed to our feeling of being in slow motion. Waiting for helicopters to airlift us somewhere would sometimes take a day or more, and that type of waiting could be boring in the extreme. Being cooped up in a firebase for a couple of days was boring and almost made you more weary than before. In the infantry, men used to say that war was 90 percent boredom and 10 percent sheer terror, a definition that, by my experience, was fairly close to the mark.

Boredom gave us time to think, and in Vietnam, that was dangerous, for it was not a thinking man's war. It was a mindless activity we were carrying out, and thinking about it did not help. Some men would write, read, play cards, and resort to other distractions. One man in my company became an accomplished knitter and would make clothes for Vietnamese children. Others found different outlets, but boredom was a fact of life for all of us. Boredom is probably a constant in any war.

Boredom caused you to relax a bit, and that could be as dangerous for some as full-scale combat. One night, we had a serious commotion, and my first sergeant told me that one of our men had been found asleep on guard. There are few higher crimes in the infantry. If you go to sleep, enemy troops can slip by, kill your comrades in their sleep, and depart without any problem. One has to trust those on guard to be awake and alert. We all took turns on guard duty and felt we were protected. To violate this was serious business. Sometimes it was dealt with then and there by the troops themselves.

The miscreant was brought before me, and I had no alternative but to offer a court-martial versus company-level punishment. In his case, the soldier felt company punishment would be the best for him and asked for that. I agreed with him. His sentence was to walk point for two weeks—something I considered near a very severe sentence. However, considering the level of his misdemeanor, I felt the punishment fitted the crime. This young soldier dutifully walked point for two weeks, did not get a scratch, and never fell asleep on guard duty again. He was fully received back in the fold of his brothers in arms. All in all, a better outcome than getting a court-martial and having that blemish on his record for life. In fact, this young man became one of the best soldiers in the company and was considered by many of his fellow soldiers as a true veteran. Months later, he would leave Vietnam a solid soldier, respected and with both the admiration of his buddies and several medals.

While few of us would admit it, we were most thankful for boring periods. They were much easier to live through and deal with than the fighting, and those times helped many of us muster strength—the internal courage—for harder times. We could also use such time to catch up on sleep. Officers could get briefings, and we could all get a shower if we were lucky. Boredom, heat, filth, and routine mixed with high levels of anxiety and fear became the way we lived, our daily lot. It had become what our country was asking us to do. America was asking its young men to do all of this in the name of patriotism.

CHAPTER 24

OF SNAKES AND MEN

We were walking—slow, cautious patrols—through some true jungle with large bamboo, all types of dense tree growth, with its lush double and triple canopy, shielding the light from the ground in most areas. The scent of the jungle is unique, a fresh natural smell that neither offends nor pleases. The jungle, especially bamboo-infested areas, was so hard to hack through that it became an enemy unto itself. In such thick jungle, one did not have to worry much about being ambushed or running into booby traps as the enemy would have as much trouble as we were having just walking through the stuff.

In the boo, as we called it, there were small green snakes, indigenous to the area, called bamboo vipers, that would coil up around bamboo stalks (so named since they were the exactly the same color) and drop on small, unsuspecting prey and bite them. They had only enough poison to kill or quickly stun rodents and small animals, leaving them listless for subsequent ingestion by the little green predators. Bamboo vipers are arguably the most aggressive snakes in the world, worse than the cottonmouth moccasins in Southern American swamps. Obnoxious little bastards, just seeing them gave you the creeps. The real problem was that with their camouflage, they were very hard for us to see, but they had little difficulty in seeing us.

The battalion command section was just ahead of my company, and I could see some of them from time to time. As we worked our way through some giant bamboo, a bamboo viper dropped out of the overhead vegetation and landed on the battalion sergeant major's right shoulder. He did not even notice it, even though several troops were yelling at him. As he turned his head to the right, it bit him just below his eye. *God, I thought, what a disgusting event. Only in Vietnam.*

The sergeant major was evacuated after getting some antivenom shots and was okay in a week or so. He came back to the battalion on a helicopter resupply flight, looking none the worse for wear. We made up a green heart for him from C ration cans since you don't get a purple heart for being bitten by a snake. He claimed the snake bit him in the face because he was so ugly. We all agreed instantly. He wore his green heart until it finally disintegrated.

One morning sometime later, we were in the central highlands of Vietnam. Our unit did not operate in this region of Vietnam very often. When we did, we received lightweight sleeping bags via helicopter resupply since it got cool enough to really need them at night. This area was more mountainous and had a higher elevation than our usual stomping grounds in III Corps, the artificial military boundary in central South Vietnam that included Saigon. On our second day in the highlands, we got up, pulled in patrols, had officers' call, and got ready to move out on our operation. One of the soldiers lay there, not moving, and with his eyes wide open. Finally, his sergeant told him, as only soldiers can, to get ready. His only response was to blink repeatedly. Now somewhat confused, the sergeant asked him if he was okay, and he blinked twice. It seemed like some kind of code. So the sergeant asked him to blink three times if he was in some kind of trouble. Three frantic blinks ensued. Now what? Was he lying on a mine or had he accidentally pulled the pin on a hand grenade? We knew enough to know this was no joke, but figuring out what was going on was our next problem.

Someone had the good sense to ask him to blink again if there was a snake inside his sleeping bag with him, and he did. That was it. In the cool of the night, a goddamn snake had gotten inside his warm sleeping bag. *High or low, this country is full of snakes.*

One of the guys who was from a rural part of the States built a small fire at the foot of the bag and slowly increased the size of the fire. Then he edged the burning wood forward, toward the soldier's head and the top of the sleeping bag. The trapped soldier was soon sweating profusely, probably as much from fear as the heat. We saw the head of a deadly krait stick out of the open end of the sleeping bag, inches from the soldiers head, and slide back inside. The krait is a member of the cobra family and dispenses a neurotoxin poison from its fangs for which there was not an effective antidote. kraits were called two-steppers by the troops—you took two steps, lit up a cigarette, and died after a krait bite. Cobras were not seen by our unit, but we did see a krait from time to time and were universally terrified of them. The M16 was a good defense, and our antidote of choice.

Slowly but surely, the krait crawled out of the bag and went a few feet away, far enough for someone to kill it. We sent the soldier back to base camp via an observation helicopter to rest for a day or so.

The sergeant who had detected something unusual and had the good sense to act responsibly and well was given a field promotion. Well deserved for saving a life. A battalion commander could promote a sergeant a rank, say from E-5 to E-6, and put him on track to becoming a senior NCO. This was not done often, but it was a true system of meritocracy and seemed to work well. Bravery, leadership, and sacrifice merited this type of promotion. This sergeant was a good example of what type of person we wanted to get more responsibility and succeed.

CHAPTER 25

A LINE OF SWEATING INFANTRYMEN

We were moving toward the Parrot's Beak, a lovely place (known to harbor major enemy units) in War Zone D. An area with triple-canopy jungle where light struggled to seep through the overhead foliage. Even in the middle of the day, it was barely light at ground level, and the days were noticeably shorter. On the positive side, meager sunlight limited the growth of underbrush, giving us good visibility, and making our movements easier. Dank and wet, this type of jungle was foreboding, almost evil, and placed a higher level of apprehension in our minds than normal.

The night always appeared more formidable in the deep jungle. Moisture dripped off the branches almost all the time, and there was seldom a hint of a breeze. Insects swarmed, and every step had to be examined for mines, snakes, or anything that appeared unusual. The trees were so high that if you called for or fired artillery, when it came in, the fuses on the tip of the artillery shells would hit the branches high up in the trees and detonate. Sometimes this could be a couple of hundred feet in the air. When this happened, the artillery (the explosions) were usually quite a bit off target and sometimes directly overhead. Air strikes were equally hazardous because their accuracy was severely inhibited. In such a situation, we knew we could not likely call on these mighty and normally reliable allies, saviors of ours, for assistance.

On the second day of this particular operation, we were up on a plateau, and the jungle suddenly gave way to an open stretch of ground, with waist-high savannah grass not even a hundred yards away. I was standing on the high portion of the plateau and looking over the grassy plain ahead when I took in the whole beautiful scene ahead. What a sight to behold. Before me stretched a long line of sweating, toiling infantrymen burdened with heavy loads and moving off into the unknown. I looked at them: young, bright, and full of life. I knew many would die in the battles that probably lay ahead. Yet these men represented the best the United States could offer. They chose not to go to Canada. They chose to do what their country asked of them. They were in Vietnam, fighting a dirty war.

For me it was an incredible moment of high emotion. Tears came to the corners of my eyes, not tears of sorrow or revulsion, but a feeling of immense pride. These were the same men who held fast at Bastogne, who seized Iwo Jima, the same men who, against all odds, struggled at Valley Forge, in the Argonne, and who all believed in their cause, blue or gray, in our own terrible Civil War.

I could only marvel at the quiet, often desperate courage of these men. Valor, in the infantry, is a difficult thing to define. A soldier who goes out on patrol at night, returns to the unit in the morning, and moves out with his buddies throughout the next day is surely a man of great courage and stamina. Even two-man nighttime listening posts, only a half mile from the main portion of the battalion, were a challenge to those who had to perform such lonely and frightening duty. Yet no man ever refused. Men quickly learn who they can depend on in war. Unlike images often portrayed in the popular media, there were no bands playing in our war to give us courage and make us stout, and no women were watching their men be brave. There were no stirring songs; there was no national fury for some dastardly attack like Pearl Harbor. What we had was the valor of the desperate; there were no heroic antics, no desire to do the unthinkable. We were more calculating and careful, an inhibition prescribed by this emotionless type of war and the way we were fighting it.

When possible, I would go on listening patrol or other patrol activity just to keep in touch and ensure that things were going okay. A listening patrol simply went out to a fixed location usually anywhere from a few hundred meters to a few kilometers from the battalion. Once in position, you would set up for the night and listen for enemy movement. You took cover but did not dig in or prepare firing positions. If a listening patrol heard anything, they were to report via radio and not fight unless they absolutely had to. Being so small, combat with a larger force would almost certainly spell doom for a listening patrol. Combat reconnaissance patrols were the hardest—you went out to find the enemy and fight in order to keep him off balance and unsure of where we were. It was also a way to bleed the enemy and cause him to lose confidence, thinking the Americans were everywhere. Usually, a combat recon patrol would pounce on a smaller enemy force and wipe it out or hit a larger force and retreat quickly before they had time to regroup and come after us. Patrol activity is one of the daily chores, the essential activity of a combat unit. Good patrolling can keep the enemy off balance and keep your own unit aware of where the enemy is and what he is up to. Patrol activity is a deadly business, and a large proportion of the casualties in the infantry occurred in these small grim, unglamorous actions.

I also liked everyone in the company to know we all shared common dangers. I saw medics stand up and go to the wounded in a hail of bullets and could only think, *May God let him live.* Countless acts of bravery that would astound a casual observer were our common lot. When a man went down, his friends would do almost anything to save him, to get him out so he could have the opportunity to be taken to a hospital via helicopter. They did it because they knew others would do it for them, part of the unspoken bond of comrades in war, and because they loved their friends. We all depended on one another. The helicopter pilots would brave almost anything, sometimes knowing they would not make it, and sometimes they did not. Artillery forward observers were always in the thick of the fight with their antennae, locating enemy mortars and calling in artillery even on top of us when it was necessary. This happened rarely, and only when a unit was overrun, the idea being that the enemy would be up and running around and the American defenders would be in foxholes or the like and have some cover from the artillery.

Then there were the infantrymen who walked point—that lead person, the first one in the line of march of a larger unit. He is out there all alone, the very first target or the first one to find a booby trap or be seen by a sniper. Someone has to walk point; someone has to do that frequently lethal job. Every day there were volunteers.

These men, the best from America, were being killed in horrible, extravagant numbers. Their bravery was, to me, a signpost of the strength of America. The battalion commander had recommended me for the Bronze Star for Valor for the second time. I had been in a sharp engagement and led the flying shit squad to destroy an enemy mortar position. I had already refused to accept a Silver Star recommendation, feeling it unearned, and the frivolous way medals were being lavished on officers who were simply doing their jobs discredited their value. In the overblown emotional environment that was ours, we would not always make the best judgments about such things. However, at the time, medals were low on the esteem ladder for I had never once walked point. Bravery is a very subjective quality, one that is valued and observed with caution by us. I had recommended two men for the Silver Star, and both had received that very high medal. Both had exhibited great personal bravery in spite of our difficult situation.

The line of men before me in the savannah grass are the ones who will make the country work. They are the citizens who will carry the load for others. They will be taxpayers, volunteer firemen, churchgoers, builders, and parents. They are solid citizens, the stuff a country is made of. They are the future of America.

I admired these men. They went about their business, while to a man, they wanted to go home. But they were here, and they went out on patrol. In combat, they charged into enemy positions. They fought at night. They carried more than their fair share in this war, and they were few in numbers, those in the actual fighting. To me, these men represented a national resource and one that was very much worth saving. Even if it required that I use up every cell of my brain. It was the most important mission, to do everything in my power to save all of these men, at least as many as possible. It became my duty, my obsession. The war was becoming an abstraction. Saving their lives, if possible, became the focus of my efforts, my most vital mission. It was the only sensible thing one could salvage from this war. Survival and returning to the world.

Every move, every firefight, every patrol, every artillery plan, all of our actions had to be considered with infinite care. *These men must be saved.* I could not accept that another soldier would die needlessly, carelessly, if there was anything humanly possible that I could to prevent it.

I found it harder and harder to accept death under the conditions in which we were serving. Each time there was another casualty, I asked myself what we could have done to prevent it. Could a different formation have been used? Called in artillery fire sooner? What had gone wrong, and who was at fault? I rationalized by saying that in war, there must be casualties. That is a truism. I still could not accept it as a fact. Not for my men. I felt that if I worked hard enough, covered all the details again and again, surely it would be enough. We would let the enemy make the mistakes.

Still, the letters had to be written, the letters back home to their loved ones, telling families that their son, husband, or brother was no more, that he was dead and had died fighting valiantly for his country. It was difficult for me to try to make such a loss as acceptable as possible, knowing all the while that this type of loss was never acceptable. My veneer of control that had kept me from imparting the true feelings of what we were experiencing was slipping. That their men were being wasted, that human life was being squandered was too brutal a message to send to a mother. It was simply too cruel to do even in this cruel war.

Those who sent us—politicians, anticommunists, and the like—had not done their job well and could not seem to understand the truth or even want to see what was unfolding. Perhaps they were simply unable to change what they had set in motion in that far corner of South Asia since an undertaking of such a magnitude gains its own momentum. Clarity afforded no balm. The longer we remained, the worse our predicament. We were on the equivalent of a fool's errand. But there was no way we in the infantry could reverse course and opt for something else.

CHAPTER 26

WATCH OUT FOR VC

We were in the soup again. Nothing big this time in the overall strategy of the war, but it was another firefight and both big and potentially deadly to each one of us involved. At last, some sensible people, somewhere in our leadership echelons in the sprawling, massive military headquarters in Saigon, or the equally massive ones in Hawaii or the Pentagon were starting to get concerned over casualties and the impact they were having on the course of the war. The word was now out from the higher headquarters: don't get soldiers killed needlessly. Use all the artillery and air strikes you need, but save the troops. I could only thank God that at this point in the war, in late 1967, some sanity was finally taking hold, even though we soldiers had been practicing such conservation on a very personal level for a long time.

My radio call sign (the military gives you an anonymous name partly for security and partly to make communications more uniform) was Vindicator 6. The tactical field radios we used had a fairly limited range capability, normally around five miles but usually not much more. At my level, I had a great need to communicate to the platoon leaders, my forward observer, and the battalion commander. We lived and died by those radios. The radio was sometimes your only link with the outside world. The radio-telephone operator (RTO) had standing orders to replace the expensive batteries daily because of the absolute need to have the best communications we could. Dead batteries could easily mean dead men. The military controlled frequencies and published them in small booklets. We changed frequencies daily, but at least we usually had good communications.

Conversations were limited strictly to business, and everything was abbreviated to make conversations as short and terse as possible. This also limited enemy intelligence from gaining too much information about you. Things could go wrong if too many others got on the radio net you were using and started jabbering. Once too many people got on a net, you could not hear anything clearly, and the system quickly became overloaded with comments and answers out of sequence. I could understand that a brigade commander may want to find out from his battalion commander what was going on, but sometimes intrusions into radio communications all the way down to the company level were both dangerous and unnecessary. With strike aircraft coming in to bomb, or artillery firing close to you, it was very important to stay in close contact with those fire support elements and all other parties concerned, especially the platoons nearest the artillery or air strikes. If you did not coordinate those actions very carefully, your own people could get killed by friendly fire, and the whole situation could degenerate into a deadly type of street brawl.

The range of field radios on the ground was not great, but being in a helicopter vastly improved the range of the radio and power of its transmissions. Ironically, this allowed someone in a helicopter or airplane (not in the ground fighting) to almost always get their communication through. Their elevation made such a difference that they could actually overpower a radio on the ground. Being airborne and above 1,500 feet also offered protection from what was going on down below. That somewhat peculiar situation of perspective, communications and safety from on-high got to be a problem for us more than once.

One day, with my company and another company from the battalion engaged with a small force of Charlies, my battalion commander was orbiting over me in a helicopter, giving me generally welcomed advice. He was a good solid commander who basically knew the score and shared our hardships. The brigade commander and brigade operations officer were also screwing holes in the sky, hovering safely overhead in separate helicopters, and providing me with advice. This advice was more remote and less useful but tolerable. And under circumstances like this, it was at least understandable for these three senior officers to be where they were.

But it went downhill from there. I was in a firefight on the ground with no less than six backseat drivers in helicopters overhead offering advice. I could only grin and bear it. In addition to my battalion commander and the brigade commander and operations officer, joining them now and orbiting were the division commander, his operations officer in one helicopter, and the III Corps commander in copter number 5. Next came an unfamiliar general from Saigon. These lofty leaders of the day were soon joined by some other ranking general from Saigon who flew in and saved the situation in the nick of time. I was receiving advice over my valuable radio net from someone (a general from Saigon) who had probably never been in ground combat or in harm's way. This Hannibal of his day had my radio frequency and was tying up my net, as were the others. On my now overloaded, crowded radio net, he undoubtedly heard me screaming orders to platoon leaders and the forward observer. We needed artillery fire right then, and we did not need help from anyone, especially unwanted meddling. It was during these critical moments that I received the following advice from the new airborne Hannibal from Saigon: "Vindicator," he said, "watch out for VC."

That was it. As most of us were every day, I was tired, sweaty, nervous, had chronic diarrhea, and was in a fight and a foul mood. *People were trying to kill me.* That has an amazing way of focusing your attention on the relevant. The last thing I really needed was some senior idiot from Saigon telling me something as obvious as the nose on your face. My irreverent response was immediate and visceral; I shrieked at the top of my lungs, *"Get off my goddamn net, you idiot! I'm in contact (with the enemy). Do you think I'm watching out for fucking Santa Claus?"* My explosion generated an immediate response: one of the more than half-dozen helicopters in the aerial circus) above us abruptly broke away from its lazy orbit and departed to the east for the comfort, luxury, and safety of Saigon. A few weeks later, I received an official letter of reprimand—for showing disrespect to a senior officer. I let every man in the company read it. Amid much hooting and laughter, we collectively took it for the bullshit it was. Anyway, what could they do to me? Put me in the infantry and send me to Vietnam?

At least the idiot got off my net.

It was months later that I learned through the military grapevine that officers from Saigon would often fly out over some infantry unit in contact, shout out some meaningless orders over the radio (like watch out for VC) from the safety of a helicopter flying high, and then go back to Saigon and bedeck themselves with medals for "saving a unit in combat" with their "clear and insightful direction and quick grasp of the tactical situation." I thought again that it was little wonder that we were in such trouble, if indeed what our higher ranking officers were doing was becoming medal mongers. This reinforced my dislike and mistrust of medals or at least of the people who collected them without earning them. How officers in the U.S. Army could do such things was appalling to me as an army captain. No wonder the average soldier had contempt for senior officers. Medals are supposed to validate real-life bravery. Again, here in Vietnam, my experience was at odds with my preconceptions. I could not help but wonder how anyone could wear a medal gained via such a manner. This was mental and moral corruption of a high order, especially in view of the fact that we were not getting the kind of honest, soul-searching effort from seniors in Saigon that should have changed the direction of the war.

A few days before the watch-out-for-VC episode, I had been on Nui Ba Den, the geological oddity known as the Black Mountain, near Tay Ninh in War Zone C. Nui Ba Den was a solid granite mountain, jutting up out of the flat terrain of Tay Ninh Province, reminding me somewhat of Stone Mountain, Georgia. During the day, Nui Ba Den almost always has a white cloud right over the top of its crest. There was a special forces outpost on the top of the mountain, and I had gone up there for some business (meeting with officers there to plan defenses and how we would come to their aid if they came under serious attack) and to generally look around for orientation purposes.

Here I met an old friend from airborne training days who had earned a reputation as a gun dealer, and he had a World War II grease gun for sale. This was the famous .45-caliber, short-range submachine gun used by Patton's tankers and others. It had few moving parts and really looked like an old-fashioned grease gun for cars, hence its nickname. It was reputed to be a great weapon in the bush: it was short, compact, with a magazine that could hold twenty bullets, and the magazine extended straight down, which helped you hold the weapon. I knew the .45 pistol was excellent as a close range weapon and thought the grease gun would be as good if not better. Both guns used the short but powerful .45 bullet. If someone was hit by a .45, they went down; there was never any doubt. So after some serious bargaining, I traded a CAR-15, a short-stocked airborne version of the M16, for the grease gun. *What a deal, I've really come off well in this trade.*

I never liked the M16, which was the standard weapon issued to all U.S. Army units. It was clumsy, hard to handle, and did not have good ergonomics. In an earlier firefight, my M16 had jammed—a little sand had done the dirty trick. An infantryman never forgets a weapon that fails, especially so easily. There is simply nothing like the click of a trigger, instead of the explosion you expect to have. The M16 was still relatively new, and it was not held in high esteem by infantrymen. Many of the troops in my company were carrying instead the fine Soviet AK-47 assault rifle. I had fired the AK a lot, and it was an excellent weapon, rugged yet with good handling capabilities, never jammed and was easy to clean—most of us thought it was superior to the M16. The danger in this was, of course, that since much fighting was at night, you frequently fired at enemy tracers which were green. Ours were red. If you had an AK, you had to fire Soviet-made ammunition, and the only safe way to do that was to strip out the green tracers if they were there. Of course, nothing could be done about the sound, which was different from an M16, but many were willing to take that chance. In a few months, we started to get AK ammunition made in the U.S., ostensibly for the South Vietnamese Army (called Army of

South Vietnam or ARVN). We used plenty of it for our adopted and trusted weapon of choice, our captured AKs.

A few weeks earlier, we had a mechanized platoon operating with us in Southern Tay Ninh Province; an armored personnel carrier had run over part of a rice paddy dike (mud wall). A small cache of weapons was discovered in the dike, including a mud encrusted AK-47. One of the armored troops took the AK by the barrel and slammed it against the hull of the personnel carrier, knocking off most of the mud. He then moved the operating rod back by pushing it in a not very gentle way with the heel of his boot. We were all watching when this soldier then shouldered the AK, pulled the trigger, and got a solid burst of fire! We were astounded at the reliability of that weapon, especially when we compared it to the overly delicate M16. The Russians had learned in World War II not to make weapons that could not take the beating they would get in hard situations, and their AK could take a lot.

At any rate, I now had my grease gun and was ready for action. I had four clips (magazines that hold bullets) and loaded them with the ammunition my pal at Nui Ba Den had given me and carried them in my web gear. Several nights later, we were getting some isolated rifle fire from a tree line near where we were located for the night. We thought the VC might have a light machine gun or two, but we were not sure. I moved up to the edge of our position, spoke to some of the men there, and got into firing position. I eased my grease gun forward and took careful aim, then slowly pressed the trigger and cut loose at the next muzzle flash I could detect, sure I had effectively hit the enemy position.

The results stunned and almost killed me and everyone around my position. It looked like I had a napalm hose or a Roman candle since a large red stream exuded from my gun. The enemy reacted immediately and with tactical skill. It seemed like every VC for miles and the entire North Vietnamese Army were opening up on me. I hugged the bottom of the foxhole for an eternity. Bullets whistled over us, some thudded into the earthen lip on the foxhole I was in. Some overhead branches got cut out of trees, and bark and leaves rained down on us. Infantrymen near me were not too kind in expressing what they thought of my contribution to their safety by attracting so much fire. One seriously irritated grunt said, *"Sir, why don't you go back to battalion headquarters and do some captain stuff and leave this shit to us?"*

After beating a hasty retreat to my company headquarters position, I pulled out a clip to see what the hell was going on. It took only a moment to find out that I had all tracer ammunition, no regular ammo. Normally, infantry would not use tracers in a weapon like that. Even machine gunners would sometimes strip them out of belt-linked ammunition. Tracers were designed to let a machine gunner see where he was firing, and he could then adjust his fire accordingly. I had fired off some fifteen to twenty tracers and illuminated myself as a target, which got a predictable response. It had been a stupid mistake on my part, not checking the ammunition. I'd fired the grease gun in various training cycles back in the States and was still quite familiar with it, so I had not even bothered to test fire the gun I acquired. I always felt lucky that I did not get killed or wounded for that mistake. Some soldiers were killed for a lot less.

Anyway, .45 ammunition was not always easy to come by. Ammo resupply was mostly M16, hand grenades, and grenades for the M79 grenade launcher. Usually, only a little would be in any resupply since it wasn't used much, and for some reason and at the time, it was almost all tracer type. I was not going to fire tracer bullets again! Plus the .45 bullets had a nasty habit of tumbling when fired from an observation helicopter due to their low muzzle velocity, so I soon traded my grease gun for a shotgun. I thought the shotgun would be as effective as the grease gun, perhaps even better, and without any undue attention from tracer bullets. I had to go to special efforts to acquire ammunition, but with that problem temporarily solved, I felt that I had found the most useful weapon possible. Armed with a high-quality semiautomatic shotgun, I felt in some ways like I was back in the central Florida scrub brush hunting deer, only now the deer could shoot back.

I would soon give up the shotgun since getting resupplied with ammunition became a serious problem, and the shotgun shells were hard to carry—too bulky and too heavy—and you could not carry enough of them. I next traded the shotgun for an excellent knife. I acquired another CAR-15 from routine supply services by the time of the Tet offensive. My weapons shopping and experimenting days were over. I resigned myself to using the M16 or the shorter version CAR-15 or an AK when I had the chance. Of course, as an officer, I continued to carry the famous .45 pistol as a sidearm, which was standard issue for officers.

All through my tenure in Vietnam, I witnessed a lively trade in various weapons. Soldiers made it a full-time hobby, and some actually had a business of supplying various types of guns and ammunition. Guys in combat units would seek out anything that they thought would give them an advantage. Some would be suckered; some would find their own solution. I had a machine gunner in my company who would not use any machine gun but the one he had had since his first day in Vietnam. He regarded it as a good-luck charm. He cleaned the gun so well and so often that he wore the finish off the metal, making it look like polished new steel. He was, without a doubt, the best machine gunner I ever knew, and he went home without a scratch after his tour was over. Perhaps this proved something, perhaps not. At any rate, simply watching the vibrant weapons trade was almost comical to me, although I never got much of a laugh out of my own experience with the grease gun.

Christmas of 1967 had just passed, and we were about to enter the New Year's truce period. These truce periods were often marked by heavier fighting than normal, or so it seemed to us. They were truce in name only, a sick joke like so much of the nomenclature of this war. Again, nothing was what it was supposed to be in Vietnam. We had bivouacked in a forested area that was actually kind of nice. Large trees with almost no undergrowth, it was dry, clean, and offered no indications of enemy presence.

The battalion operations officer and I struck up a conversation about the coming New Year. We both wondered if we would see it through and jokingly pondered what we would be doing next New Year's Day. We could not focus on the immediate future, only that distant, abstract future much further away, too far ahead to plan on but fun to speculate about. This seemed to be fairly normal for the infantry since it was a reflection of our day-to-day existence, reflective of our inability or unwillingness on our part to face the dangerous near-term events coming our way. A month seemed like a lifetime away, and a week was a long time off. We measured and experienced time differently.

Little did we know then, but in less than a month, we would be embroiled in the most savage and deadly fighting of the entire Vietnam War.

The battalion operations officer declared that he planned to be in Las Vegas next New Year's and would celebrate there with his wife. I thought this was a little odd, but he responded that it was a desert area, with lots of lights and entertainment, nothing at all like Vietnam, and that alone would be cause for celebration. I could not have agreed more. I told him that I would like to celebrate the next New Year's Day in Florida, and even if it was a cold January day, I'd still take a swim in the wonderful surf of Daytona Beach, Florida, and enjoy the sun. We spent much of the evening reflecting on what life in the future would be like, especially space exploration and the possibilities that offered for the future scientific advancement of mankind. We offered our opinions on whether or not NASA would actually land a man on the moon and bring him back as President Kennedy had envisioned. Odd, that in the most destructive endeavor in which mankind engages, two infantry officers would be concerned about future scientific advances for the good of humanity.

CHAPTER 27

TET, BLOODY TET

After being in Vietnam for eleven months, many things, the things of war, had become second nature to me. Eleven long months in combat is a long time, each month seemingly a lifetime experience. Eleven months **was** a lifetime in our compressed experiences. Intuition started to augment training, and it revealed why soldiers who are old soldiers become more effective than ever before. Training only opens certain avenues to you, but combat experience teaches those who live through it. Training and intuition became blurred, but those of us with a few months experience shared what we could.

I was a seasoned veteran, an old battle-hardened soldier at twenty-six years of age. The Old Man, that is what those with less time in-country called me and the other experienced company commanders. I accepted the nickname with amusement and a dash of pride. Of the 140 men originally with the company when we left the States, only 88 were still with us. The others had been killed, wounded, and sent home, and a couple had been transferred to other units. The war was indeed going on too long.

Many of the men in the company, especially the noncommissioned officers, were older than me. Age is a strange thing in combat. Younger soldiers take more risks since they are not yet aware of their mortality. This recklessness does not last too long, however, and they become cautious, careful, and more experienced soldiers. Mostly, age made no difference to us at all; we simply all looked alike, acted alike, and that was enough.

We had returned to operating in War Zone C, which perhaps had now surpassed War Zone D as the most dangerous and troubled of the war zones. The enemy seemed to prize War Zone C more as it was a direct route to Saigon and wanted to keep it open for his supplies. War Zone C was familiar to us; it was our special place in the war, our hunting ground. The war zones were areas in Vietnam where everyone (every Vietnamese) was considered hostile and could be engaged on sight. There were few civilians—they had all supposedly been resettled, but we knew some had returned to their ancestral homes and farms and were scratching out a living in a very dangerous part of the world. In the war zones, we could use all our artillery and air if we needed it without prior clearances. In some ways, this was approaching the conventional war so many of the American military officials longed for and tried to force on the Vietcong and North Vietnamese.

As soon as we settled in and started operations again, we could hear Charlie moving at night every night. The clack and rattle of men and military equipment on the move is distinctive and unmistakable. Your ears become as well trained as any part of your body, particularly at night, and we were hearing a lot of enemy troop movement. That scared the hell out of us since we were deep in Indian territory. We set up ambush patrols and sent out combat reconnaissance units designed to find the enemy and fight every night. Every day we moved and patrolled, looking for Charlie. But something was very, very different. I went out on a listening patrol myself to see if there could be another explanation for these atypical activities. Again, there was movement, but it was dedicated and with a distinct purpose. The enemy seemed bent on moving east, and there was little we could do to interfere. We were dutifully reporting this information up our chain of command to higher headquarters.

At first and at our low level, we could not figure out what was happening. We were all perplexed. Normally after contact, Charlie would fight furiously for his weapons, his wounded, and his dead. He would even clean up the area if he could, so as to leave no clues, hints, or trails. Now something was different; Charlie was not picking up his weapons. He was even leaving the wounded and dead. We had seen Charlie fight to the death to accomplish these goals before, but now they appeared to be of little value. This was not the Charlie we knew so well. He was up to something, and we all knew it. A weapon was a valuable commodity, almost priceless to a poverty-stricken army, yet there they were—even machine guns and ammunition—alongside the dead and wounded.

We were not in some large headquarters or in a comfortable command center location in Hawaii or Washington. Still the average grunt knew something big, something 180 degrees out of normal was going on, and it was a very worrisome change. Infantrymen know that change, especially change like this, rarely means anything good. Most soldiers had a sense of foreboding. Some few felt like this was something new and exciting, others said, "Just another fucking day in Nam." But we all knew something very strange and probably very big was up.

In the weeks just before Tet, we were sucked right up to the Cambodian border, like most of the other American combat units in Vietnam, forming a loose barrier to keep the South safe by interdicting the Ho Chi Minh trail, which ran from North Vietnam, down through Laos and Cambodia, and into South Vietnam. Contact continued to be light, with only the odd enemy behavior of the past few weeks being distinctive. Then we were suddenly put on high alert and told to be ready to move.

In moments, we received emergency orders at about 10:00 pm the night before Tet—*move to Saigon! Saigon! What the shit is going on?* That was where all the staff and rear-echelon weenies were. *Saigon!* That was the capital of this place, the nerve center of the American war effort. *What the hell were we going there for?* We would all find out soon enough.

Some few units went by helicopters to a site close to the city, the rest, including our battalion, began a grueling road march. Mines, ambushes, traps, snipers, and the threat of assaults by major ground units made the trip to the Saigon area a hellish nightmare. We had to fight our way past our old initial staging base at Cu Chi since it was on the road to Saigon. North Vietnamese regulars had set up road blocks, and large enemy units were marauding through the countryside, wiping out small detachments of U.S. advisors and isolated units. As soon as we got past Cu Chi, we could already see tracer fire arcing up into the air, leaving trails in the sky over Saigon some fifteen to twenty miles away. Fires were burning out of control all over the city. There was heavy fighting; we were racing toward an inferno. All the U.S. radio nets were full of those crying for help.

The Tet offensive was under way.

Still some miles away from the center of the city, I heard a senior officer who had found our frequency and was on our radio net. He had identified us as an infantry unit, and his call was to order us to come save the personnel in the BOQ (bachelor's officers quarters) where he was located and secure the building. They (the BOQ) were not too far away, but in the confusion, it was not clear that we could get to them in time. Worst of all, there were no weapons at the BOQ, and the officers there could not even defend themselves. They kept the radio net open. We could hear Charlie come in the building and methodically go from room to room, slaughtering them all. Later we would learn that there was an enemy regiment between our position and the BOQ, and almost a full day and a half of fighting intervened before we actually got there and could verify what had happened.

When we finally reached Saigon, we started operations out of a place called Hoc Mon, a suburb with little in the way of distinguishing features. After the first day of trying to sort out what was going on, we got orders to head for the Phu Tho racetrack, destroy any enemy along the way, and secure that area that would be used for helicopter resupply and medical evacuation. Now the level of fighting was the worst I had seen so far. Men in the battalion, including my own company, were dying in outrageous numbers. We could not move without being attacked, sniped, shelled, or otherwise engaged. The enemy in large numbers was everywhere. We were hemorrhaging to death. We were killing many of the enemy, but that did not matter to me. I was not able to eat for a couple of days due to constant movement and the high tempo of operations we were on and got only fitful moments of sleep.

The fighting continued night and day for three weeks. Furious, horrendous, and without mercy or letup. The point man, lead man in the unit, was killed instantly the first time we attempted to press on to the Phu Tho racetrack, which was our initial mission. Nevertheless, we made some progress toward the racetrack. Saigon had buildings that were made of concrete and not unlike those found in small U.S. cities. On our journey that we assumed would take no more than an hour or so, we came to a large intersection with five— and six-story buildings on all corners. As we approached the intersection, I had my company command group out front; we were expecting no immediate combat contact as this area was secured by South Vietnamese troops, and this seemed to be the best way for my company and the battalion to proceed.

At the intersection, we had to make a right turn; and as we came to the edge of the building and were preparing to go right, we literally bumped in to a North Vietnamese unit. They had the same company-sized headquarters out front including a couple of officers, some men with radios (you could see the antennas), just like us.

I saw what appeared to be the man in charge, and our eyes met. We were about twenty feet apart. Both of us froze. We all eyed each other, knowing that if anyone on either side made even a small move, we would be enveloped in a deadly, terminal duel. I did not know if their unit was the head of a battalion, regiment, or a full division, and they did not know our strength either. Looking at them, seeing the fear in their eyes, and the sweat on their faces, they looked like normal people, not our enemy. I knew (all of us knew) that death was only a flinch, pulled trigger, or grenade throw away. It seemed as though we eyed each other for fifteen to twenty minutes, but I am sure it was measured more in seconds. Without direction, the North Vietnamese and we started to take little steps to the rear. Then almost imperceptibly, both sides disappeared behind the large building. Then we both deployed, and the fighting began anew. It was one of those unbelievable moments in war that one seldom hears about, but it was real, vivid, and put us a millimeter away from death and wounds.

My lead point man was killed, and he was the second man to die in this manner. He was replaced, and the process was repeated (the next man was only wounded), and then we began to get enough momentum to dislodge the enemy who had effectively pinned us down. The air seemed full of hot, jagged metal, whistling by and letting us know how close it was. The grim reaper of death was having a holiday.

Casualties bleeding red, those of us left alive to continue fighting were white with rage and frustration at our predicament. Too many men were dying. The operations officer I had spoken with—about the next New Year and what we would be doing once we were out of Vietnam—was shot through the neck by a heavy machine gun bullet and died mercifully fast. Next to be killed was the new medic who was married and had a small child. His death was particularly sad for me, in that he died painfully with his hip and lower back torn to shreds. He knew he was dying and said so. He asked that we not summon a medic and that his last letter home be mailed. He could not bear to risk the life of another medic. I submitted this brave man's name and deeds for the Silver Star, which he so richly deserved. He was posthumously awarded the medal a month or two later, and it was sent to his widow.

Madness, insanity. My god, when will this end? My radio operator helped me get into my gear after a brief rest and never said a word. He knew that I was sinking like a ship into a deep sea of desperation. Struggling in to the harness for the day's work was approaching the impossible.

War is a brutalizing experience, and it dawned on me early on that some of the people doing this dirty work were not altogether sane. One man in particular, Sergeant Jimenez, was a classic psychopath. He would ask to go out on patrol by himself and come back with a bloodied uniform. I discovered that he sometimes went out only with his entrenching tool (small shovel), which was razor sharp, and would return only at first light. Jimenez liked killing; he told me so face-to-face with a Richard Widmark-type grin during a discussion I had with him. He was an excellent soldier, but I wondered what we would be releasing on the American public if he got home and started practicing what he had discovered in Vietnam. My fears on this score were put aside during Tet. Jimenez took three machine gun bullets square in the upper chest near his right collar bone, blowing out a softball-size hole in his back. He died in seconds. The loss of another soldier was unfortunate, but strangely, I hardly mourned for Jimenez.

Unknown to myself and the rest of the officers in the battalion, he had collected the ears of enemy troops he had killed; he would cut them off dead Charlies and keep them in an ammunition holder on his web gear. This form of sadistic mutilation was not only disgusting, but it would have gotten him in serious trouble had it been revealed. From other experiences, such as his going out on patrol by himself and coming back with blood on his uniform and his obvious delight in killing, I considered him a homicidal maniac. This one particular situation had resolved itself. I do not believe anyone really knew what he was doing or the extent of his illness since any responsible person would have put a stop to it quickly.

The Kafkaesque nature of what was going on was unbelievable. We had an entire regiment of North Vietnamese troops surrounded near Saigon's Tan Son Nhut airport. We had five U.S. battalions—it was no match. They were simply slaughtered. They died slowly and to the last man. We sent in interpreters to ask the last few to quit and surrender; none would. *Fuck it.* They were shot on the spot as troops could find them. This was not the time to fool around or try to be too generous. This was deadly serious business. Casualties were such that no one felt particularly kind. Malevolence was in the air. Troops from an American mechanized unit, particularly hard hit, had lost all their officers. Only a few sergeants were left. They were losing control both as a unit and individuals. When a small isolated group of Vietnamese decided to surrender, or at least walk out toward the Americans, one of the soldiers from the mechanized unit sitting on top of an armored personnel carrier opened up with a big .50 caliber, literally cutting the fifteen or sixteen Vietnamese to pieces. I guessed actions such as these were all part of the unspoken rules of war. I realized again, as I did nearly every day, that there was no glory or adventure in the infantry. Killing humans is an ugly, horrible business.

Watching the Vietnamese soldiers being shot down, their intestines flying in the air, half of one head came off a body, and blood splattered in the air, I felt like it was all a bad dream. My world became almost gray; a cloud of insensitivity closed in over me. Any notion of glory, duty, or fighting for anything but survival was being shredded. I was becoming emotionally void; I was feeling less and less. I wanted to shut my eyes to what was going on and close my mind to the sights I knew would last a lifetime. One Vietnamese I saw was hit in the head with a heavy machine gun bullet, and his head exploded like a melon. Others were just shredded and died.

Meanwhile, the fighting went on. The enemy came at us in enormous numbers not like the few Vietcong we were used to seeing. These were regular army units attacking us, and we were cutting them to pieces. Saigon was now a ruined city. We did not really care if we blew down a few more blocks here and there, so our firing became somewhat less discriminate. Soon the rats came out. Fire drove them from their nests, and they were all over the place. I had lain down in a small one-man bunker near Hoc Mon to get a little sleep since my first sergeant thought I was so groggy that I was becoming dangerous. After a few hours' sleep, I was startled awake by a noise outside that I could not identify. Instinctively, I assumed it to be enemy sapper troops. I slowly took out my pistol and cocked the hammer. In the moonlight, I saw my enemy—a large rat in the firing aperture of the bunker. Terrified at the prospect of close combat with a rat, I slowly pointed and fired. I'm sure I killed the rat but did not think about the consequences of firing a gun in a closed space. I was deafened for a week and was amazed that our tunnel rats, the soldiers who regularly went down into tunnels looking for VC, had any hearing ability at all. During this time, officers were allowed and encouraged to kill all animals on sight since rabies was reportedly becoming rampant, and Saigon had plenty of dogs, cats, various pets, and an overabundance of large rats. To add to our nervousness, shots now rang out at odd times as dogs, various pets, and vermin were shot when detected.

I had not slept for about three days and was so exhausted that I could hardly function with any degree of clarity. It was like being in a slow-motion state. Everything I did was slower and cloudy. My first sergeant finally told me to lie down and sleep for a while since I was getting dangerous. So I found a place and bedded down with a promise to be awakened if anything happened or after four hours, the maximum I felt safe sleeping. The very next thing I knew, I was being shaken awake. Top said I'd been asleep almost five hours. I felt somewhat refreshed and started to look around but could not get oriented. Finally, I asked Top what the hell was going on, had we moved, and I did not know it or what. He then told me that we had been hit with about two hundred rounds of heavy mortar fire and that most of the flimsy buildings had been blown down or badly damaged. I'd slept through the entire thing and never heard a sound!

Gradually, after almost three weeks, the fighting died down somewhat. My unit, my battalion was shot to pieces. From some 900 men before Tet, we were now able to muster about 365 men for duty (called effectives in military lingo), perhaps less. Many men were lightly wounded and would return later, but those badly wounded would go home or at least be flown out of Vietnam for more extensive medical attention. It was unlikely we would see them again. Many were dead. Some 2,800 Americans had been killed in the first week of Tet with casualties almost as high for the next two. The fighting would then lessen as enemy casualties soared to unacceptable levels, and they ran out of what meager supplies they had.

After Tet, I became the senior officer in the battalion for the amount of time in-country. I did not feel senior, but I did feel increasingly weary. After Tet, I wanted to go home, to get out of Vietnam and forget what it represented. I was not the gallant hero that I'd dreamed of in my youth, nor was I the protector of my family and country. No bands were playing; there would be no victory marches back home for us. We had no support from the home front. We were fighting a hollow war, and we knew it. After Tet, my mind kept repeating, *They sent us. We pay the price, and they could care less.* This was not an exercise in self pity, but a gnawing painful truth about America's war in Asia.

We were tattered enough to be pulled out of action and left on the outskirts of Saigon to lick our wounds and receive replacements. The fighting up in the North, at Hue especially, seemed heavy and more prolonged than what we had experienced. My heart went out to our marine brothers who were bleeding as we had been. In my soul, I wanted to join them and help, as we had helped our comrades in central and South Vietnam; but on the other hand, I could not bear the thought of more men in the unit dying.

I thought of the sacrifices I had seen over the past few days, the courage of men who wanted just to live and get out of Vietnam and go home. I still could not understand the practicality of what we were doing, but I knew we were doing it wrong. You cannot help people by killing them. You cannot teach democracy at the point of a gun. I wanted to leave that place. But I couldn't, not yet.

Our souls were being pulled in two directions. On the one hand, I wanted to win the war and get it over with. However, what we were experiencing was far from a war worth winning. I was somehow glad for television back in the U.S., for it was showing the war with stark clarity. I had seen a newscast once at Cu Chi on a TV in one of the command centers.

Replacements also told us about the evening news and the impact it was having on the public. On the TV screen, you could not lie or cover up, and slick briefing officers could not explain how everything was really okay. Even though I felt the press was against U.S. involvement in the war and by definition was against us and actually aided the enemy by putting them in the best possible light. I knew some of the things I read in newspapers from home were crap; nevertheless, some truth had to leak through. I did feel that the American public had a right to know the truth. They were investing their sons, husbands, and fathers. You can never withhold the truth in a democracy, nor should you try. Our truth was savage, sad, and terrible, but it had to be told; and as imperfect as the press was, it **was** telling the story of the war. There was probably some built-in bias against the war by the press, but then a large segment of the U.S. was against the war, so where was the truth?

After a few days' rest and refit, including getting some badly needed replacements, I took out a patrol to rescreen an area near Phu Tho. While we were out, I took a spent bullet in the back, which hit the muscle area and lodged on my left shoulder blade. I was sent to one of the hospitals in Saigon, where medics took out the bullet with a long probe. It hurt for a while, but I was very thankful that the bullet had no energy left, and I had not had my shoulder shattered or worse. I got a good night of sleep in the hospital, a shower, and rather decent food. It being a minor wound, I was back with the unit the following day but would return to the hospital in a few days to get the stitches removed and receive an antibiotic shot to guard against infection. My unit personnel viewed my getting hit as a badge of honor. Many of them had been, and they liked officers that shared what they were experiencing.

Tet had shattered our unit, and for me, a lot more had been broken. I felt spent and now with a physical scar to accompany the emotional damage I had sustained in the weeks of desperation, futility, and waste, which was now called Tet. In the U.S., the antiwar element was in an uproar, with demonstrations at an all-time high. Even those who quietly supported what Johnson was doing now had their doubts. President Johnson was losing popular support even more, and the rot of what the Vietnam War represented was beginning to show at home and on the battlefield more and more. I knew we would lose the war, and many more of us would lose our lives in the process. This fact was a pity. We should pack up and leave. Tet was my high-water mark. I no longer had any confidence in our leadership. As far as I was concerned, they were bankrupt and did not have the vision to end the war or win it. I no longer cared about the goddamn war; I just wanted to get my men and myself the hell out of there.

CHAPTER 28

A FRIEND DIES

Steve had been my radioman for a long time. He carried the heavy field radio, spare batteries, maps, and extra smoke grenades to guide helicopters in to landing zones. When he was on leave (the famous R & R), his temporary replacement had been killed. Perhaps it was the nearness and unpredictability of what could happen, the constant presence of death and mutilation that bothered us all. The strange steps and missteps of fate, part of guerrilla war, danced a macabre minuet through our minds. Steve, though, carried his concerns quietly, without much obvious distraction. Once when he was hit in the leg by a grenade fragment, Steve stayed in the field with only a bandage dressing so he could carry my radio. Fearing infection, I made him take an evacuation helicopter for treatment, and it was during the week or so he was gone that his temporary replacement was killed.

He was a cheerful young man with a quick wit, and you could tell he would probably be a success at whatever he did after the war. He always had batteries for the radio and carried extra rations since I frequently forgot mine or was at officer's call when rations were passed around. Steve always had the field maps ready, sometimes would prepare my foxhole, and, in general, made my life a good deal more bearable. He was smart, and he could tell by the anxiety in my eyes when things in the bush or in my head were not going well. He had a real talent for doing that; he read people well. He was also the mail clerk for the company, so he knew more about what was going in the lives of all of us than most and, in small but important ways, kept me well informed about things I needed to know. If somebody got a Dear John (usually a letter from a girlfriend or wife saying they had found someone else), they would bear extra watching so they did not do something stupid, like trying to get killed while depressed. He was no spy or anything like that, just good common sense and an uncanny ability to sense things and understand people. He put these talents to good use in our situation. It was like having a good psychologist along with you. I held his comments in high regard and usually found what he said to be of value.

Steve used to take care of our little company headquarters cell, usually about five of us, counting the forward observer and his radioman and my first sergeant. He volunteered for any tough job and always did more than was expected of him. More than once he carried ammunition during heavy combat to men who were running low and helped wounded get to incoming evacuation helicopters. Perhaps his best asset was a positive outlook. Even in tough times, he always had a smile and good cheer to pass on to those more troubled than he was. He was not flippant or some kind of featherweight, but he considered it part of his job to make everyone else feel a bit better. This young man said he wanted to drive race cars when he returned home.

He was destined never to make it. One night, an undetected Charlie hunter-killer team got in near our position. They carried rocket-propelled grenades—the infamous RPG-7—and other powerful weapons so as to inflict the maximum number of casualties on the Americans. Already the Vietnamese knew the effect casualties were having in the U.S. and their devastating impact on the American war effort and public opinion. That psychological/political effect was worth a great deal to them. They were willing to incur heavy casualties just to damage us a little. The Vietnamese knew they did not have to win the war; they just had to not lose it.

We were almost on the edge of the battalion perimeter; our positions were about fifty feet from the actual firing line. When the shooting started, I thought little of it since it was not too heavy. We had the situation well under control and were keeping the enemy at bay with artillery and our own return fire. However, unknown to us, two Vietcong had crawled through our line with an RPG. They were looking for a worthwhile target, which usually was a group of careless men who clumped together. They had to know they would be killed as soon as they fired their RPG. The worthwhile target they chose was our infantry company headquarters so marked by several antennae.

Steve saw them just as they were kneeling, aiming, and preparing to fire the grenade at our company headquarters antenna farm. Without thought for his own safety, he simply yelled, "Sir!" The RPG grenade, which was designed to knock out a tank, was fired and came flying toward us. Steve was about ten yards out in front of our position, and the rocket hit him right in the chest, detonated, and blew him into a thousand pieces. There was not enough of his remains for a body bag. I always felt he could have moved, and the rocket would have detonated elsewhere and probably killed most of the company headquarters. But I had seen him protect us before; I know what he did.

We did, of course, kill the VC team that had come in to our position and fired the RPG. Their action cost them two dead and us one. Another futile little engagement that would not mean a thing to either side in this war; it was just simply killing for the sake of killing.

I missed Steve very much, and it was difficult to think about what his life would have been, what kind of person he would have become. His death had a profound effect on me. The grief I felt was for the sacrifice of a fine young American. Our sacrifices formed a brave backdrop for a terrible drama of waste. Another letter home. Another family in agony. Since I could no longer steady my hands enough to write, I dictated such letters to my first sergeant who wrote them clearly, and I signed as legibly as possible.

I do not think that I can go on. At least I knew that I could not continue like this. I was utterly convinced that this war had to end; we Americans had to do things differently, better. I could never return to Vietnam again, never, but there were officers who had already had two or three tours of duty here. It was becoming a treadmill, an endless cycle of violence, death, and fear.

I had made a dreadful mistake and violated one of the cardinal rules of true soldiers. I had gotten to know a fellow soldier well. We were all people who thought others would get killed and wounded. Not us; not me. I knew Steve, had heard about his family and friends, where he went to school, and how he grew up. I had grown quite fond of him; he was something like a younger brother. In war, one does not need friends. They die. It makes the entire process more difficult.

It is better to see a shattered unfamiliar body—simply another soldier, a faceless body—rather than a friend who happens to be a soldier. If you know someone better than just a name, it turns the morbid task of writing a letter home to his family into a gruesome event filled with recriminations, bitterness. Officers can be lonely people. From then on, while I would get to know others, it would be at the most superficial level possible, nothing more. It would prove far easier for me personally, and it lessened my liabilities as an officer.

CHAPTER 29

MURDER FROM THE SKY

Andy Jackson, the outstanding artillery forward observer, was dead. Al Kennedy, perhaps the best platoon leader I ever knew, was dead. Too many others, like Steve, were dead. Many more were hurt, shattered in body, spirit, or both. Mental clarity was escaping from my psyche as internal doubts reached a crescendo in the back of my mind, questioning my rationality. I was having more difficulties focusing on events at hand: it seemed hard to concentrate on those things that needed my attention. My eyes would lock on to objects for long periods of time, almost glazing over. I was not in deep thought, just a blank haze, a type of mental void where I did not have to deal with the events of the day.

In my own cocoon, the solace of thought free from an insane war was my escape mechanism. Food was of little interest except when necessary, and my weight had fallen to a mere 128 down from 175 upon arrival in Vietnam. Everything drifted across my mind as irrelevant. Not much seemed to matter anymore, except nice days, and those were the days without fighting. Once I took sincere care about my own physical safety, a thought that seemed totally ludicrous now, especially since it was taking more energy each time. I was not unique; other men too seemed to care a lot less now than when they first arrived here and were initiated into the infantry. Earlier I felt it was heroic to survive and go home, having abandoned so much of my initial thinking. This much still held true. *I have always assumed that someday I would return home, but I was beginning to doubt even that. Nor did it seem so important anymore.*

Much of my former edge was gone, and many of the men around me were simply going through the motions as well. It was a narcotizing effect that too much time in the war had on us. We were experiencing combat fatigue.

Still, rage overpowered apathy and indifference. War is in fact hell, to quote Union General Sherman, and I knew that when nations clash or even societies, that soldiers would die in numbers and ways only they can understand. The young men of my era had been psychologically and physically prepared to fight the Third World War. It was to have been an extension of the second one. Instead, our clever enemies had lured us into a sophisticated trap, and we were now locked in a war that we could not win. In fact it could not be won. Even if we did win, what would we win? Their political leaders had outthought ours, but our soldiers had outfought theirs. What this meant was that we would still lose the war. We could only apply the tactical expertise and superior weaponry and soldier skills. Nevertheless, we would continue to bleed and win those engagements. But the cost was becoming prohibitive.

On the other hand, the North Vietnamese and their allies were winning the propaganda war around the world. In short, while we were winning the war on the ground, the North Vietnamese realized that this did not matter, and that they would ultimately prevail.

Tricked, lured, squandered, wasted, irrelevant were no longer mere words, and they danced through my mind like a ballet, but to the music of Mozart's "Requiem."

I wanted to strike out, to get revenge, to hurt Charlie badly. I noticed that an observation helicopter had just landed in our position early on that hot Vietnamese summer day, the morning after Steve had been killed. I spoke to the pilot and ordered him to take me up on a reconnaissance mission. In the small fixed wing observation aircraft similar to Piper Cubs, we had a technique of getting as much altitude as we could, then cutting the engine to its minimum (some of the more daring pilots would cut the engine off), and then gliding as long as possible. This was not feasible in a helicopter, but if you were high enough and going slowly, it was hard for Charlie to hear the engine from the ground, and the aircraft was also hard to see. We were doing this when I spotted three of them, enemy troops bicycling along a trail. I already had artillery ready and on call, and it was a simple matter to get an air burst of six deadly proximity-fused 105-mm shells right over them. Which I did. The blooms of the artillery detonations looked almost like harmless temporary flowers near the ground, not betraying the violent killing process they were.

I directed the pilot to land on an open spot close to the now-prostrate bodies on the ground. He was hysterical with fear and expressed his opinion that we would be killed. I think he was a little bit more afraid of the dangerous, depressed, angry armed man sitting beside him, so after a bit of time, he landed.

The war had reduced my psyche to one of morbidity. I wanted simply to see their bodies, witness their death. I needed to inflict pain on them, on the enemy, to compensate for the pain in my soul, the pain of the infantry. I picked up their bloody guns and threw them in the helicopter, and we flew back to the unit. Neither the pilot nor I spoke on the flight back. I took the AK-47s to the intelligence people so they could add the three I had killed to the infamous body-count tally of secretary of defense William McNamara. This was the supposed proof that we were winning the war. I thought I would feel better killing enemy troops, but I did not. As soon as I left the tent where the intelligence people were, I saw the blood on my hands and promptly threw up behind another tent.

Simple manslaughter or pure first-degree murder? Yes, I was angry, beside myself with rage at losing another man. Furious at what was being done to us and the injustice we were experiencing. *The best of America is bleeding to death in a fucking jungle, and nobody is concerned. Were the protesters right? It does seem crazy. What the hell are we doing here? What are we supposed to be doing?*

But we are here. Goddamn it, at least we can fight our way out, kill enough of the bastards so they leave us alone or we win.

I thought, *Is this what I have become?* A leader of dead men, a killer from the sky? I had killed three men in cold blood, not in the heat of battle, not in some great campaign. Three more dead on a trail with no name and for nothing. I rationalized that it was war, but later I could not make it stick in my mind. I did not have to do what I had done to save myself or my men. Somehow there was a difference, and I knew this would be another lifelong scar. I am not a murderer. That day, I made the business of war the business of my own need for revenge under the guise of war.

My ability to think clearly had become elusive, no longer a constant. The need for a long rest or to go somewhere, anywhere there was no fighting, no more leadership, no questions or decisions craved inside like a fasting appetite. I didn't want to be involved in fighting ever again. Life is too precious. Some people could do this. Some even seemed to enjoy it, but it was tearing my guts out and eating me alive. I simply could not handle this war anymore. I wanted to quit; I had had enough. My war was over. I began to think that life had a peculiar way of piling trouble on when you were down.

Two days later, we were marching through some tall savannah grass, which was usually anchored in a viscouslike muck. The strong blades of savannah grass had razorlike edges that could shred your skin if you were not careful. We came into an area where the grass had been burned by some previous fighting and was a lot shorter. There were clumps of hammocks or small points of land a foot or two above the water table that supported tree growth, each a mini-jungle. Another American battalion just ahead of us was in contact and had called in air strikes.

One of my soldiers well ahead of me as we were walking along was suddenly decapitated as in some ghastly circus act. This was a daytime nightmare, and a fountain of blood shot up from his body into the air. He had been hit by a large American bomb fragment. The fragment was the square plate that holds the bomb to the aircraft and was supposed to shred into small pieces of shrapnel, but it did not. This large twenty-pound piece of metal came flying through the air for over a mile and took this young man's head right off. He was killed instantly.

I helped look for the fragment, wandered off to a small secluded area. There, amid the razor-sharp grass, I threw up from the bottom of my soul, vomiting so violently that the physical demands of standing or catching a breath were out of reach. I thought I was dying. I was helmet down on the ground and could not move. After a long time, the medic came over and put smelling salts under my nose. That simply made me throw up again, but the chemical jolt was strong, and I got on my feet, and with his help was under way. It was not just the death of another soldier, but the entire insane business that was going on. *God, please stop this war.*

We then went into flanking action to relieve the battalion ahead of us in contact with the enemy.

Another young soldier was now my radio operator. I wondered how long he would live and reflected on the disregard with which I viewed replacements and how that made their lives even more difficult. Antennae attracted attention since Charlie knew it usually meant an officer was there, so I was not sure this new radio operator would see the end of his tour. I simply could not dwell on it or think of what might happen, much less what had happened. I now compartmentalized my mind, living from moment to moment in a world that I did not want to know and could no longer understand.

CHAPTER 30

ONE MORE TIME

It had been weeks since I'd been able to process the turn of events in our world. It was difficult to reflect on what had been happening, not that many of us really wanted to think about it all that much. I had reached a point of numbness, a dull awareness, but nothing else. Yes, I could still do what was required, but what I did was rote. Many of the troops who had been in-country too long had a blank stare like mine, and their eyes would fixate on some object for extended periods of time. In World War II, it was called the one-thousand-yard stare. In World War I, "shell-shocked" was a term used for the state some of us appeared to be in. Some of my mental references were now in the third person—"What would Vindicator do?"—things like that. We were in a shroud of doubt, cloaked in the mystery of the meaning of our war. We were men simply doing what we had to do. What terminology would future generations coin to call our combat fatigue?

It had been more of the same, those last few sad weeks. Casualties, small in number, big in impact. One day, one of our patrols crossed into an unmarked South Vietnamese minefield, and an American soldier stepped on a mine, which blew his leg off above the knee. I remembered when our unit was carelessly shelled by a South Vietnamese unit some months ago and could not help but think, *With allies like these, we don't stand a chance.* According to regulations and common sense, minefields were supposed to be carefully marked; engineers were supposed to record exactly where the mines were and keep the information for use when needed. This was especially helpful when moving through your own minefields or when you had to remove them at some later date, like when the war was over. But the South Vietnamese had not done anything except indiscriminately seed antipersonnel mines about. These small plastic encased mines were not as powerful as a grenade, but they could blow your foot or leg off. They had no wire or prong protruding or any type of sign that they were there, and they would last a long time. With even the firing mechanisms being made out of hardened plastic, the mines would withstand humidity, rain, and decades of weather, only to detonate under the foot of some unsuspecting adult or child. We all had our special hates and dislikes, and I especially hated mines and snipers.

Our unit was worn out, exhausted. We had two days off back at our old familiar Dau Tieng base camp. The remnants of the old French plantation provided a familiar backdrop, some bit of comfort for everyone. At the officer's club, there was a small swimming pool and a snack bar that served cool but rancid-tasting South Vietnamese beer. Simply being out of the firing line seemed a little like heaven. Like most unit commanders, I had seen to it that my company had been billeted, fed, was getting new uniforms, and was taking care of weapons—all the normal things we did when returning from the field. At about noon the next day, I went over to the little pool and swam a while, then had a couple of those terrible Vietnamese beers and started to think too much, so I decided to leave the pool area. I must have looked odd, even for Vietnam—helmet, rifle, brown army-issue boxer shorts, and flip-flops.

I had to cross the airfield runway to get back to the area where we were staying. It was a typically hot day. The stroll was pleasant, and there were no duties pressing, nothing one had to do. As soon as I got out near the middle of the runway, the familiar whine of incoming rockets shattered the lazy afternoon. They were the big ones, 122-millimeter Russian rockets that struck the earth with bone-jarring ferocity. This was the famous Katyusha or Little Kate of the Second World War—the Soviet rocket that had shattered so many German units. The rockets were landing everywhere, and some were coming right up the runway not all that far away. My only chance was to make a run for the other side of the runway since there was a drainage trench some twenty yards or so away that would give me some cover. *Goddamn if I was gonna get killed or torn to pieces during my last few weeks.* The edge of the runway neared, I kept going and flew into the ditch and felt immediate pain. Lying there, hugging the wet dirt, half in water, and praying that I didn't get a round right on me since if that happened, there wouldn't be enough left for a paper bag. The pain, which was now centered in my groin, soon gripped my thoughts like a vise. My fears were for shrapnel in that ill-protected area, but fortunately, that was not the case. In my frantic sprint, I had pulled two groin muscles and would limp for weeks.

We were scheduled to go out again on another operation two days later. The night before, we would draw ammunition and prepare as usual: officers' briefing on the mission, map distribution, flight plans, what helicopter unit would be supporting us and taking us to the battle area, what artillery units would support us in combat and their fire support plan, locations of all friendly units were plotted, where we had to get permission to fire—all was carefully noted. The troops drew all the ammunition they could carry along with first-aid pouches. First-aid pouches would be the first thing a medic would use on you if you were wounded. Not to carry one was to take a needless risk. The average soldier always cut straight to the chase.

Dawn crept up on me; the morning air was pleasant and fresh, and I could hear sounds of the base camp. For months,

I had been awake in an instant. Sleep, when it came, had been evasive and not satisfying, just a pause in the routine. Now on the morning, when I should be up and preparing to depart on one of the last operations before departing for home, simply getting dressed was beyond me. My mind was a complete fog, an absolute and dense haze that could not be cleared or shaken. Concentration was impossible, except for fleeting moments. Lost was my ability to struggle into the harnesses of war, something I had done with intensity months before. Sunk in this stinking reality, my own private hideous war, reality was retreating from me. There was no future. My hands now trembled so badly I could not load my weapon or get my web gear on, and it was obvious.

I was billeted in a French two-story house. I was sitting on the steps, and the battalion commander came over. He said, "I hear you don't feel well. Why don't you go on this operation and take a few days off when we get back."

So within the hour, collected enough to continue, I had boarded the command helicopter and headed out with the battalion on the operation. I compartmentalized everything now. It was a simple matter to separate what I had to do, what I saw and experienced, and what I wanted to do. It saved the mind from too much torment and allowed you to function at some level, maybe not quite as good as before but at least function.

The compartment in my mind now said "fight," for we were heading out to do just that. The area we were about to operate in had been full of enemy recently, and there would likely be a lot of fighting. The whole thing smelled badly in the age old lingo of the infantry.

Nevertheless, the search and destroy mission was mostly search. With very little enemy contact, they had gone. We came back to our base camp, and it felt almost as if we had not gone out. It had become so routine and mindless. After a couple of days off, which were strangely unrefreshing, we heard from the news in the U.S. that the Reverend Martin Luther King had been murdered, and this deepened our moods. The war, this rotten war was the problem, not an extra day off. It was something we did not know how to address.

While we were back at Dau Tieng, an administrative officer came over and told me that I was due to rotate out in a month or so. In my compartmentalization of things, I had lost specific count of how much time I had left, even though most men in the bush knew their time remaining down to the hour. I was dimly aware, though, that the end of my tour was near. He also told me that I would not be eligible—would not have to go back to Vietnam—for twelve months. However, if I signed up for six more months, I could not be sent back for at least two years. This was the reward for signing on for eighteen months (a tour and a half). Infantry officers were now at the point of spending one year in Vietnam, a year home, and then back to Vietnam. At this point in time, I could think of nothing worse than going home, waiting a year, and coming back. If I ever left, returning would be difficult, if not impossible.

I thought about the company of brave men that would be left behind. Leaving these men to another officer, who may not be seasoned or worse may be a careerist or lifer or, even worse, an inept officer who would be willing to sacrifice the lives of these men to look good and get a promotion quicker haunted me. The prospect that they could be wasted by some glory-hunting idiot bent on making a career out of slaughter was upsetting and did not seem fair, but in this case, there was nothing I could do except trust that the army would select a good officer and that he would do well.

Many of the original group of men I had come to Vietnam with had already departed, one way or another. But their replacements were here, and it was sometimes hard to tell the old guys from those who had been around for months. I wanted to see all the remaining men I brought to Vietnam go home. With very mixed emotions, I signed the dotted line and extended for six months to see them home and leave Vietnam once and for all.

CHAPTER 31

THE SHOT HITS HOME

The next few weeks were little more than a blur, the monotonous routine of patrols and enemy contact with the inevitable results. I had been in Vietnam for seventeen months now, and with a little under a month to go, I actually felt numb, bored, and empty. War is never depicted as monotonous, but it can be and arguably was much if not most of the time. One evening, back up near the Cambodian border, we were under a fairly heavy attack just after dark. I decided to go to the battalion headquarters, get an idea of the overall tactical situation, and find out if my company should be prepared to counterattack if there was an enemy breakthrough. I told my first sergeant what to prepare for, then got up out of the bunker, and headed for the battalion command post.

There was a bright flash, like a momentary glimpse at the sun. Then it was dark, a deep dark in the unusual sense of unconsciousness. My next sensation was cold, a terrible type of cold, one that seemed endless, like a long black tunnel. It was a cold one could not find the end of, one that did not seem normal. In such a deep darkness, one does not have conventional memories, but there were hallucinations. There was a feeling of falling, hanging on the side of a cliff, not having enough strength to hold on, and letting go. Other hallucinations were as bizarre and as realistic. One had to do with a school teacher who kept a machine gun on her desk, ready to fire on any student who did not sit at attention.

I had suffered a glancing blow to the head, one which caused a lot of bleeding, and rendered me unconscious. At night, with lots of blood from the head and other places and with a low pulse, I was tossed on the "meat pile," an infantry term for where dead bodies were placed. Luckily, someone saw me move sometime later, and I was subsequently evacuated on a medevac helicopter.

My first real memory was of someone fooling with my eyes; the mystery hands seemed to be trying to open my eyes and shine a light in. A faint voice noted, "We have eye movement." I had been unconscious for about two hours, perhaps more. It was hard to tell unconsciousness from exhausted sleep. We all snatched sleep whenever possible, and in all probability, being hit and being tired crossed. Under the circumstances, one should be grateful for the sleep. Medication also played its part, and the morphine sulfate I had been injected with blurred my ability to sense time and turned my unconsciousness into a veritable walk down a very peculiar yellow brick road.

I had few sensations, and it was not clear at all to me why my surroundings had changed or where I was hurt. By now, however, I realized I was in a military hospital. Something was wrong, dreadfully wrong. My new habitat was too clean and quiet, and the sounds emanating from various quarters were not those of war or even those that had a faint ring of familiarity. Strange sensations began to emerge; my teeth and jaw seemed to throb with an unusual hurt—much more painful than a toothache—and my ears were ringing loudly, even worse than after being exposed to gunfire. I could not smell but thought nothing of it at the time. The movement of the helicopter, which I had been evacuated in, still held my balance, like the feeling you have after being on a ship for a day or so and still feel like you are on the ship even though you are on dry land. All of these sensations came cascading in on me, but my mind could not sort them out to any specific conclusion. I was in a time-out.

In the recent past, there had been people yelling, voices saying incoherent things; I heard firing and then a simple nothing. Clean clear nothing, no dreams, nothing but absolute deep nothingness. I had been down for the count but was now witnessing a jumble of half-sense and all-too-true reality. The new battalion medic had given me a strong painkiller for insurance against me thrashing about or even sticking my fingers in the wounded area.

I had been taken to the main evacuation hospital in Saigon. There, slowly, ever so slowly, things started to return to a semblance of normality. Vision, that incredible tool of the senses, was blurred. Smells still did not register. My ears were ringing louder and felt like cotton was stuffed in them. It seemed like something was in my eyes, but the outline of a nurse appeared dimly through my right eye. I asked her what was wrong with me. I thought I had stepped on a mine, or maybe some type of booby trap had gone off. She said both legs were there, but I did not believe her. I learned later it was common for nurses to lift up legs of soldiers if they were there, so she lifted both of mine, and I got a fuzzy view of them, one at a time, enough to put my mind at ease. I had always dreaded mines and snipers—two very insidious ways to be killed or maimed. I remember being so very tired, a fatigue unlike that of the past, and so sleep, exhaustion, and fear of the unknown closed in on me for an undetermined period.

In retrospect, I think the coldness I felt initially was probably due to the altitude of the helicopter since when it got to over a few thousand feet, the temperature started to drop radically. Most evacuation helicopters flew well above the range of heavy machine guns and other antiaircraft weapons. My enforced inactivity may have contributed as well.

Some hours later in the hospital, I was dimly aware that I was coming around; the fog was lifting a little. I knew I was in a hospital and had both legs. What I still did not know was why, what had brought me to a medical facility. I knew I had both hands. I could feel and see them, so I then checked certain male vital spots and found all was okay there.

I found that I still could not see clearly. Even though I could see both my hands and had moved them in front of my face, I began to understand that something had happened to my vision, especially my left eye. It is a human fear, deeply seated, being blind or even losing an eye, and I knew my eye had been shot out. To be blind has its own unique horror. I touched the side of my head and found out that my suspicions were well founded since I could feel a large bandage or wrapping all over the left side of my head and more gauze and plaster of some kind that went down my back. The morphine had started to wear off. So apparently had the side of my head.

Meanwhile, I was evacuated to the neurological ward at Camp Zama, Japan. The flight seemed fairly brief and most of us were medicated to ensure a smooth trip. Gurneys whisked us to our new domiciles, and we did not know it then, but we were to join a long treatment queue.

The doctors came in sometime later during my first full day in Japan. They wanted to operate on my left jaw. The doctor/surgeon said they would go into the jaw area from in front of my ear to the bottom of my jawline to repair the broken bone in my jaw. I knew the kind of scar it would leave, and I really didn't want to deal with a large zipper on the outside of my face. I implored them to try to do it from the inside. They agreed after a long discussion and did go in from the inside and spared me the appearance of a large external scar, a favor I have always regarded as kind if not gentle. Since then, I've often thought about the funny or odd things one worries about in such a situation. In retrospect, I should have been glad to be alive and not worried about the cosmetics of an operation. My wounds were not that severe; I would recover.

My eyes were bloody, and my jaw was broken in several places. I learned to eat through a straw with my teeth wired shut; it was a novel experience for a while. The medical people told me there would be permanent but minor eye damage and some loss of hearing. As an officer however, it would not be enough to keep me out of combat in the future. A ligament had been stripped away from my spinal column, and a vertebra had been fractured in my upper back, along with a fractured skull and twenty-seven stitches in my scalp. I was told this would all mend, the luck of the young. There were quite a few pieces of shrapnel embedded in various parts of my body, but the largest ones were taken out by the doctors then. Others would be taken out later.

The enemy had fired a captured U.S. 106 mm recoilless rifle shell, which had glanced the left side of my helmet and hit a tree behind some distance behind me. The explosion apparently drove me into the ground, breaking my jaw and doing some of the other damage. I will never know the exact sequence of events, but I think my head was thrown violently to one side, causing the damage to my vertebra, and then the detonation of the shell when it hit a tree well behind me blew me forward as I was falling down. I was a very lucky man. Many others were not nearly so lucky, as they were literally torn apart in the violence of combat. The irony of being wounded by an American-made weapon captured by the Vietcong did not escape me.

Lying helplessly in the hospital, waiting to mend, I missed my unit and the men I knew and wanted to see live. I hated what was happening, but I wanted to go back to the only home I knew. Daily, I grew more and more confused. It was a troublesome period filled with ambivalence. In the hospital, I could watch some TV and see the demonstrations, the politicians, and the process of America ripping itself into factions. Some malevolent form of evil seemed to be at work, something we could not understand at our level. Some sinister force had put the country on a collision course with itself; I could not really understand the ramifications of all of these things and where they were headed. On the one hand, I felt like throwing in the towel and simply walking away from the war. On the other, I felt I needed to go back to my company. Actually, I simply wanted to go back. It had become my family.

Was I addicted to the thrill of war? Was it the camaraderie? I could not really tell what was pulling me back, why I wanted to go. I hated the thought of losing the war after all our sacrifices, but even that was not it. I could not put my finger on the real reason. It was there, like a magnet, drawing me back, back into the unknown, back into the valley of death. I knew what awaited me, and like a deer with its eyes fixed by the light of an onrushing car, I saw what was coming at me.

In my hospital bed, I was flat on my back and quickly became bored. I found that each ceiling tile had twenty-seven dots in it. The air-conditioning came on every eighteen minutes and ran for approximately six minutes. I counted the rust spots on the bed frame, fifty-three as I recall, and I memorized the meal schedules and soon knew what each tray would be. I captured medical information such as my own chart, X-rays, medical literature, and the like when possible and became slightly conversant with my healers, much to their mirth. I also found that beyond discussing my medical condition, I did not have much to say to the staff, and they had even less to say to me. They were not harsh or cruel, but they were efficient and very busy. It was apparent that we were worlds apart; they were healers, practitioners of the Hippocratic oath, and we were destroyers, presenting an almost insurmountable chasm in itself. There was a frustrated anger about them, and even the superficial babble about weather and sports was largely unavailable to us. It was strictly business.

I think they knew that much of their work was wasted, for those lightly wounded would go back to combat—some of them to die or to come back wounded to the same hospital. I think many of the medical people were alienated simply by being in the military and being in a position of serving for the Vietnam War. Most had no choice and were conscripted right out of medical school. Having to deal with the carnage of the war firsthand was having a major adverse impact on them. I think they did their absolute best, even under those trying conditions, but they had their own torment and anger. I sensed their anguish and felt more sympathy for them than they probably did for the wounded. Years later, I would view *M*A*S*H** episodes on TV in a somewhat different light than most people and probably enjoy them more.

After my hospital stay in Japan, there was a fairly long period of physical rehabilitation, which was in an area adjacent to the hospital. At Camp D, there were specialized treatment facilities and all types of care. One clever soldier said there were lots of medical facilities in Asia because the military did not want the U.S. public to confront the cost of the war by seeing so many wounded troops. The whole episode kept me physically away from Vietnam for over four months, but my thoughts were there every minute. The urge to go back was compelling. I wanted to go back; I felt that things were incomplete. I had not completed my tour with my company. Too much was left undone. It would not be right to just pack up and go home.

My unit had become my home; the jungle was my yard. Some of the troops used to say, "Stay near Captain Elliott 'cause he don't get shot." I sure proved them wrong. But the urge to return was compelling, and I prepared to do just that. Reflections came pouring in.

In the kind of guerrilla war we were experiencing, you felt that every weapon, every enemy soldier, even the weather and nature itself were all after you personally. Everything had your name on it. In Vietnam, we experienced a very intimate, almost personal form of warfare—snipers, mines, ambushes, small violent actions. The feeling of isolation was pervasive. Some men developed a sense that everything was against them; we had no home front, no rear area, nothing but ourselves and our own resources. This increased the mental stress much more than the type of combat most Americans had seen before.

It would be much later that I felt this was the true reason I had originally extended my stay in Vietnam to eighteen months, rather than the routine twelve. We were a family, alienated to all but one another. It was a unity of brotherhood.

Perhaps the worst element for all of us in danger was that we knew we were being sacrificed for little of value, simply for political arrogance and vanity in Washington, for egos that could not come to grips with making a mistake or with their transgressions. An incredibly powerful tool of American power had been wasted by a corrupt policy. Never again would people so blindly believe in their government, nor would they ever again allow the blood of their children to be spilled so freely, so capriciously.

There were many wars in Vietnam. Airmen mostly lived in Thailand and essentially had eight to five jobs, with some serious stress visited on the few hundreds of pilots who actually went into combat in their aircraft. Sailors probably could tell little difference from being off the coast of Vietnam or in the North Atlantic. Even in the army, there was a great variation. For instance, support and logistics personnel lived in large bases and had little or no chance of getting hurt. Many officers never left Saigon. The real war was with the infantry, artillery, and armored troops who were in the field. In Vietnam, most combat troops were infantry and artillery and both army and marine. Of course, some air force, navy, and marine pilots took great chances, as did the helicopter crews, but these made up a very small portion of their services. It was the infantry, as usual, which carried the brunt of the fighting and over 95 percent of the casualties.

Even in the infantry, there were something like three wars. The first was the initial involvement of U.S. forces in which a lot of special forces were employed, mostly in training the South Vietnamese, and this went on up through 1965. The second major war was the big unit phase, when large American units were fighting against the regular military from North Vietnam. It was this phase that gave us such names as the Tet offensive, Hamburger Hill, Hue, and Khe Sahn. This phase went from 1966 to about 1969; most of the American casualties were sustained during this period. After Nixon came to power, the war slowly entered its last phase and started to wind down and became a war of boredom. Units sat out their time in bases, keeping their casualties to a minimum. Some called this period the drug war. It lasted from about 1970 until all Americans were out of Vietnam in 1973.

I had not heard much about drugs and initially was quite concerned about both drugs and alcohol. I remember the first night in Dau Tieng, the evening before a major operation. I thought it wise to check the enlisted men's club and the noncommissioned officers' club to make sure not too many tied one on (got really drunk) and went to the field with a hangover. Upon inspection, both clubs were deserted; no one was there from my unit—the entire battalion—not just my company. I checked several other areas and came up empty handed. I then went to the barracks area and found almost everyone asleep, cleaning weapons, writing letters, and praying. To drink and get a hangover was to dull your edge for the next morning. To do drugs and walk point was effectively a death sentence. The men I knew simply wanted to go home and were willing to do their part to get there. This was not a college fraternity game or party. This business could kill you for very little in the way of a mistake.

It struck me then that these men were serious soldiers. For these men, this was not a drill. This was no game. This was life and death. *To fuck up was to do it once, for here you did not get a note from the teacher or a scolding from your parents. Here you went home in a body bag.* This was deadly, unforgiving business, and the people I knew took it as seriously as they could. I never once saw drugs or alcohol. I did see men examine every bullet, clean their weapon several times a day, and many would pray to God to save them. It was also ironic to me that the common soldier was doing his job and his homework better and with greater concern than the leaders of the day. It was not just Washington that had failed, but our higher headquarters had not distinguished themselves either. No brilliant strategies, even though there were new weapons and some new tactics. Most appalling was the lack of honesty. Few were the people who stood up and questioned the war, its goals and our objectives, and all the other hard questions that should have been asked. Easier to let troops die and simply fight a mindless war.

I did hear about the antics of rear-echelon troops with drugs, alcohol, and women. While soldiers will always seek out women, if available, the drugs did not start seriously until the Nixon phase of the war when everyone was sitting around doing very little. In honesty, it had probably started earlier but not in combat units, at least not up through 1969-70, when there was still much fighting going on.

CHAPTER 32

GOIN' HOME

Well, *I'll be goddamn*, I thought, *I've made it.* Not shot up too bad, still intact body, and most of soul. After rehabilitation, I took a flight back to Saigon to do a few weeks of limited duty at my battalion headquarters and finish my eighteen months in-country. The wounds I received would not permit me to go back into combat, yet I was profiled, which meant physically impaired. I was glad at last to be completing my tour and leaving Vietnam. I felt that I had given it my all and had nothing to be ashamed of. I was ready now to leave behind all that the war represented and what it was doing to those involved. My mind was heavy with the thoughts of those who left in body bags and the experiences we had shared. We had accomplished little, destroyed much, killed many, and in the process, we had all become casualties.

Just before leaving, a small delegation of men from my company who were still in Vietnam came to say goodbye and gave me an emptied-out (one could carefully chip out the brick-hard explosives in such shells) Russian 82-millimeter mortar round, now chrome plated, with "To Captain Elliott from his men" inscribed on the side. I did not have a clue as to what to say, so I shook hands with those there, trying to remember who had been with me from the start of this long, long journey. Faces became a blur, and I felt myself becoming elated at the thought of leaving. It was good to be going home, home at last. It was also great to see some these men—the men I knew from my company—finally going home too. Others had replaced our casualties, and some of our original team had been rotated with other troops to make sure the entire unit did not leave at once.

Most of the battalion was out on an operation, but my old company had come in to do the usual things in base camp. I went out to meet the new company commander. After a few minutes discussion, I gave my pistol to him and wished him luck. He would need both. I looked him in the eyes for a while, trying to sense what kind of man he was, how he would fare, how he would care for the men under him. My thoughts transitioned quickly, and all I could muster as a thought was, *You poor son of a bitch.* We shook hands, said a few more words about the state of the unit, and I departed.

The slick (a slick was an unarmed transportation helicopter—slick sides) was waiting. I got on board at the Dau Tieng airstrip, where I had pulled my groin muscles a few months earlier, and prepared for the flight to Cu Chi. When we were airborne, I looked out over the landscape of Vietnam for what I hoped would be the last time. Below were the giant scars of the Rome plows. Much of the landscape near Cu Chi had been transformed into a moonscape, like the Iron Triangle I had seen on my first flight in. We were blowing this country to pieces, destroying it acre by acre. We arrived at Cu Chi's airbase. From there, I was supposed to fly to Bien Hoa and then await the jet flight home. I waited for only a few minutes, boarded the helicopter, and we were airborne and headed toward the giant Bien Hoa base, where the airport was. We would be out-processed and then board an aircraft, just like Peter, Paul and Mary had immortalized—"I'm leaving on a jet plane."

Then just a few minutes outside Cu Chi, when we were at about seven hundred to eight hundred feet, there was a terrific explosion, and the helicopter slammed hard over to one side. *Goddamn, goddamn, goddamn,* ran through my head as I thought, *this is it.* No one lives through a helicopter crash from that altitude. Quickly, dashing through my mind were thoughts of other scenes where I had seen helicopters rotate over and crash upside down, leaving only dead soldiers and burnt, twisted metal on the ground. I am dead in my last few hours in Vietnam. *What a lousy fucking break this is.* We had all heard about the soldiers who had been killed at the evacuation center during Tet by a rocket round; that seemed to be the greatest injustice of all. Military gear, C rations, and all kinds of stuff flew out of the open door of the helicopter as we were just about at a ninety-degree angle.

I thought the pilot was hit. I had seen it before, and it was all too familiar—a helicopter would get hit, roll over, and be pulled down by the giant blades—and never with survivors. Then I saw the pilots moving as they struggled to regain control. The helicopter jerked about and pulled up. We leveled off and landed softly on a nearby road. An American artillery unit had fired just as we had gone over their position, and the shells had come extremely close to our ship. There were a few burn marks on the helicopter where the shell had gone by; it had been that close. It only takes a small hole in a helicopter rotor blade to upset the balance and bring one down.

I remembered sitting on the side of the road for a while. I could barely breathe. Then I was on my knees, hunched over again, vomiting. Afterward, I could not do anything. After everything else, this was simply the last straw; I had all but gone over the edge into the dark void. I almost wished they had hit us. *Fuck it, fuck this whole insanity, this goddamn war with its needless death and pain. Who sent us here in this ultimate folly of arrogance? Men as good as those who died should only have been sent for the most noble cause, not this idiocy.*

When we arrived at the giant Bien Hoa airbase and out-processing center, we were instructed to throw away our uniforms and set aside what we wanted to keep. Soon the MPs came to search our belongings. I felt like a prisoner being searched. First welcome back from the war? This does not look good.

I was arrested on the spot for having a weapon. Returning GIs had already established a somewhat tarnished reputation as far as taking home war souvenirs, so as usual, the military was overreacting. When I protested and pointed out that my weapon was an empty mortar round, that the explosives had been taken out and the empty shell had even been chrome plated and had an inscription on the side and was given to me as a present when I left, it fell on deaf ears. I was then escorted into an officer's room and received a lecture from a rear-echelon major, an ordnance officer with a spotless uniform, about taking weapons home. The mortar round was confiscated and placed in a pit where dangerous things such as live grenades were discarded. Engineers would come along every so often and blow up these items. Just before leaving, I could not restrain my curiosity, so I asked the major if he had ever been outside Bien Hoa, and he said, "Once, to Saigon."

Four hours later, I boarded a big commercial B-707, which could have been the very one that brought me to Southeast Asia those long hard months ago. The B-707 I boarded had brought new replacements to Vietnam and would be taking me and other veterans home. I could not help but notice and feel the American assembly line at work. In a way, it was a marvel and an astounding technological achievement. In other ways, I had to wonder at the expense and the superfluous, almost casual technique of fighting a war in such a manner. Soon the aircraft was off the runway, bound for the U.S.

Just before departing the Bien Hoa airbase, the Armed Forces Radio Network announced that 177 Americans had died in this week's fighting.

I knew intuitively that what I had done and experienced, what I shared and witnessed was indelibly printed in the landscape of my memory and would be with me for the rest of my life. Having survived the physical demands of the war, I hoped that I would not succumb to the psychological aspects. I thought, *I will heal.* I would live and try to put this behind me. I owed it to those who fell.

As the airplane soothed us with its comfortable cool ride, I started to try to write again, to try to put down some reminders of Vietnam so that I would be able to revisit them later. I had written my mother some notes about the conditions in Vietnam, never anything to make her worry, but just notes that I knew would be good reminders if I ever wanted to recall events. I knew I would never need notes to call up the alarming clarity of a firefight. I knew my thoughts of the moment should be saved, revisited, and perhaps someday imparted to others interested in what we did and what it was like for us on the business end of America's worst and most divisive war since the Civil War.

Our cause had been folly; our nation had been plunged into deep trauma, leaving America in need of repair. I did not think we would defeat the tide of communism and the Soviet Union in this manner. We would not be able to show others a better way, a democratic path by simply building better weapons and having more supplies.

We must use our collective wits, our drive, our energy to think of how, as a nation, to be the true leader of the free world more carefully. Wars have a huge psychological factor. We went to war in Vietnam without a clue.

I will always feel that Americans are a special group. We are capable of much more than we did in Vietnam. Misguided policy, poorly executed warfare, ruined public support, and no clear ideas, ideology, or aims defeated us early on. The public simply did not buy the line that we were stopping a domino effect, neither did the soldiers who bore the brunt of the fighting. Most Americans saw no value, no critical U.S. interests at stake in Vietnam, and they saw better than our leaders that the price being paid for that misadventure was too high. There was no soul in our war.

Our national failure had been monumental, and our leaders still could not grasp what was happening. The war was continuing. Their understanding was lagging considerably behind that of the general public. The war in Vietnam was not analogous to some social project back home. It required a national effort, not guns *and* butter in a casual sideshow effort. War is too serious for that. We had attempted to fight a war against communism but wound up on the wrong side in a civil war. We did not know the true issues that divided that poor country, and we were on a trajectory to failure. It could be no other way; it was the truth. Some in the military were already saying we were not defeated militarily, forgetting (or never knowing) that war is a highly political undertaking. And I knew we would lose. North Vietnam's flag would fly over Saigon, probably within days of our departure.

Political failure and breakdown, whatever one elects to call it, was also at fault in the U.S. "Others had started the war" was a phrase often heard. No one took ultimate responsibility or was willing to get to the root of the matter. The war gained its own momentum, its own cause and had patrons on both sides. In the end, not a single vital U.S. interest was at stake. Only some misguided ideas and egos were at stake, and young men paid the price.

We left behind us the souls of thousands of young American dead and tens of thousands wounded. Even those who were not physically wounded would carry scars of their own. The American military had torn Vietnam apart. The physical destruction was so widespread that full recovery would take more than a generation. The countryside was turned into something similar to a moonscape, and we had slaughtered a generation or two of their men. In the midst of this carnage, we damaged and dislocated their population by uprooting hundreds of thousands of Vietnamese people to relocation camps and making refugees out of others who simply fled to large cities to get out of the fighting. We had killed thousands of civilians unintentionally in the chaos of war. In the end, there was no domino effect, no communist wave, nothing. And we knew it.

If we are to represent America, if we are to show what democratic values are, such things as respect for human rights, value of the individual and free enterprise, we must not fall into such a situation again. We need to change our ways. Having won World War II and concentrated on the Cold War that followed, we were woefully unprepared for this unique type of struggle and did not put our best foot forward. The U.S. was not outfought, but it was outthought. We need to study our mistakes, to learn from them and prepare for the future.

Already, I knew we retained the flexibility to learn and do better. I wanted very much to work from the inside, from within the government on this issue. I made the easy decision not to throw my medals over the White House fence, nor would I join the antiwar protesters or the many who openly condemned any approach we attempted. For me, these were never serious considerations. I knew we could do better, and I wanted to be part of that effort. I would attempt to do something in the future, unclear as yet, but I will work within the system and make it better. It is after all, a good system and a fair one, and I owe that sweating line of infantrymen that much.

CHAPTER 33

LAST PATROL

The yardstick for the rest of my life,
will be the experience of the jungle.
Nothing will be so hot,
Nothing will require the intensity,
Everything will be compared to this.
The fear of walking across an open paddy,
and the sickening crack of rifle fire.
A part of my mind will always be there,
You cannot forget it all,
though blessed be the human mind
The feeling of comradeship, shared
pain and anguish will not be approached.
The experience, the will, the blood,
cannot be compared to daily life.
I was in the valley of the shadow of death.
We did not know what evil was.
We feared death, for no one was with us.
We had but each other.
We had nothing else.
Against this experience all other things
are somewhat less.

EPILOGUE

Elliott almost completely recovered from his wounds the first few months after returning to the United States via Hawaii, where he spent a few additional weeks for physical therapy. He would have continuous lifelong back pain from wounds and some minor sight and hearing loss. But recovery was excellent for him. During this time, the protests against the war were growing, and he found himself pulled in both directions. Repelled by the illogic of the war and the fact that he knew it could not be won, but unfamiliar with the protesters' methods and dubious about their sincerity and goals, he grappled with the question of which direction to take. Ultimately, he decided to work for change within the system.

During the next few years after Vietnam, he worked for the Department of Defense both as a newly promoted major, then after resigning his commission, as a civilian. He became an analyst for Middle East affairs and was one of the first people to brief Henry Kissinger on the October 1973 War in the Middle East. Shortly after this episode, he was assigned to Kissinger's staff and subsequently invited to join the State Department and began a long career there, mostly working on political-military issues in the Middle East. Elliott took part in the Kilometer 101 negotiations between Egypt and Israel, the Sinai withdrawal talks, discussions on Lebanon, two of Sadat's visits to the U.S., and numerous other Middle East negotiations.

More than once, Elliott put his career at the State Department on the line. In one of the more significant instances, he was adamantly against the ill-conceived deployment of U.S. Marines to Lebanon. He was singled out by several powerful political personalities and, in one letter, described as "not a team player." Nevertheless, his persistence, along with others who recognized that the Lebanon situation was a debacle waiting to happen, paid off only after disaster struck the marines. On several other occasions, he attempted to put his lesson of the past to good use and work from the inside.

Elliott had resigned his commission but then joined the U.S. Army Reserves and served in various capacities over the next eighteen years. When Operation Desert Storm erupted on the world scene, he was a full colonel. Activated as the commander of the Kuwait Task Force, he was in charge of planning the reconstruction of Kuwait when that country was liberated. Kuwait was restored in record time, earning Elliott the Legion of Merit. More importantly, it gave him the satisfaction of knowing much of the wrong of Vietnam had been set right at last.

The misguided destruction we visited on Vietnam was in stark contrast to what we were able to achieve in Kuwait. Most of Kuwait's citizens were saved, and very few died in the fighting. Moreover, we were clearly in the right, a just war that earned the respect and support of most of the U.S. population. It was a thrilling experience to see the U.S. Army at work, nation building and doing an incredible job. We earned the eternal gratitude and thanks of the Kuwaiti people for a job well done, for their liberation, and for our continuing support. We did this one right. The United States had regained its balance.

Printed in the United States
By Bookmasters